T0283202

Fiestas in Laredo

Matachines, Quinceañeras, and the George Washington's Birthday Celebration

Norma E. Cantú

Number 30 in the Texas Folklore Society
Extra Book Series

TEXAS
FOLKLORE
SOCIETY

Stephenville, Texas

10 9 8 7 6 5 4 3 2 1

Permissions:
Texas Folklore Society
PO Box T-0295
Stephenville, TX 76402

The paper used in this book meets the minimum requirements of the
American National Standard for Permanence of Paper for Printed Library
Materials, z39.48.1984. Binding materials have been chosen for durability.

The Library of Congress Control Number is 2024946172.

ISBN 978-1-957720-00-5 (cloth)
ISBN 978-1-957720-01-2 (ebook)

Fiestas in Laredo is Number 30 in the Texas Folklore Society Extra Book
Series.

The electronic edition of this book was made possible by the support of the
Vick Family Foundation. Typeset by vPrompt eServices.

To all folklorists who have worked in the field creating a body of work we can call Texas or Tejano folklore, especially those who have influenced my own work: Don Américo Paredes, Jovita González, J. Frank Dobie, Richard Flores, Joe Graham, Pat Jasper, José Limón, Suzy Seriff, Guillermo de los Reyes, Charlie Lockwood, Elaine Peña, Francis "Ab" Abernethy, Alan Govenar, Fran Vick, Meredith Abarca, and the many organizations like Texas Folklife and the Texas Folklore Society that support the artists, dancers, and creatives whose work enriches us all.

To all Laredoans who have worked—and those who continue to work—long and hard to make these celebrations happen.

Table of Contents

Preface

I originally encountered Norma Cantú's scholarship during my first semester of graduate school while working on a paper on Borderlands literature. I met her in person the next year at my first American Folklore Society meeting. I was a starstruck graduate student, overwhelmed to be in the room with so many of the names that had made up my recent bibliographies, when Dr. Cantú came over and greeted me. She then made a point of introducing me to a number of other folklorists. As a student from a small program, I was made to feel truly welcomed at the meeting by Norma's warmth and generosity—and in many ways to the discipline of folklore studies as a whole. I have been honored to call her a mentor in the years since that first meeting, and her scholarship has continued to be a source of guidance and inspiration. When I arrived in Texas to begin my position with the Texas Folklore Society, Norma was one of my first emails.

I can't describe my excitement when Dr. Cantú entrusted the Texas Folklore Society with the publication of *Fiestas in Laredo*. This book continues Cantú's decades of scholarship on the Texas-Mexico Borderlands, particularly her hometown of Laredo. Cantú embodies the dual roles of a trained academic and a community scholar; it's clear in this book that she has a depth of knowledge about Laredo that would be nearly impossible for an outsider to achieve. She has always had a sensitive eye for the interplay of ethnicity, national identity, gender, and language in this liminal space, as is evident in this book. While it's perhaps more academic in tone than many TFS publications, Cantú's skill as a novelist and poet makes *Fiestas in Laredo* beautifully written and easy to read.

Her concept of *sentipensante* (thinking/feeling) folkloristics draws on the concept of sentipensante pedagogy developed by another

Laredo native, Laura Rendón. Sentipensante folkloristics provides us new ways of understanding fieldwork and folkloristic analysis; rather than striving for an unachievable objectivity, it allows for the blending of intellectual knowledge with the emotional component of lived experience. Cantú shows how the three fiestas that are the focus of this book—the matachines dances, quinceañeras, and Laredo's celebration of George Washington's birthday—all reflect Laredo's unique history and Borderlands culture. Her analysis is heavily influenced by another Texas luminary, Gloria Anzaldúa, and her concept of *nepantla*, a Nahuatl word meaning "a quality of being in between" (1987). Laredo is physically located in between the United States and Mexico, but its in-betweenness is also cultural as it blends influences from the United States, Mexico, and the Indigenous communities that precede both nations. While these fiestas vary in scope—from the citywide Washington's Birthday Celebration to the more familial quinceañeras to the community-supported matachines—all of them allow the people of Laredo to explore and express their individual positions within the in-betweenness that characterizes the Borderlands.

Fiestas in Laredo builds on the Texas Folklore Society's long tradition of documenting the lore of the Texas-Mexico border—a tradition that dates to our very first publication in 1916, which features a variation of the *corrido* "Adelita" collected in Laredo. This latest TFS extra book is a fitting continuation of a legacy begun more than one hundred years ago.

The year 2022 was full of challenges and triumphs, but if there's anything that studying folklore will show us it's that the folk are resilient (and what is the TFS but a folk group?). While the COVID-19 pandemic prevented us from meeting in person, it also prompted us to find new ways to connect with fellow members. Amanda Jenkins started working in our home office in April 2022 in the varied roles of office manager, membership coordinator, and communications manager. She has been an invaluable asset, and I can't thank her enough for the help she has given to me personally and to the TFS as a whole. I also want to make sure to mention our two undergraduate interns, Guinevere Rogers and Jillian Tyler, who have helped catalog and organize our library and archival collections so that we will be able to support future folklore researchers.

I also want to thank Kay Reed Arnold, who finished her term as TFS president in the spring of 2022; Donna Ingham, who followed her as president; and Meredith Abarca, who became our vice president in 2022. Their leadership, along with that of the entire board of directors, have been instrumental in helping the TFS to thrive and grow. As always, many thanks to Ronald Chrisman and the rest of the staff at the University of North Texas Press for all of their help and patience with this publication. Finally, thanks to all of you paisanos. You are the true heart of the Texas Folklore Society and I am honored to be one of you.

Kristina Downs
TFS Secretary-Editor / Executive Director
Tarleton State University
Stephenville, Texas
July 12, 2023

Acknowledgments

I acknowledge and recognize that my work in Laredo and along the borderlands, *esa franja fronteriza* (that border strip) that lies along the lower Rio Grande, could not be possible without those Indigenous peoples who first settled here and those who subsequently passed through, leaving their mark. These groups include, among others: the Coahuiltecan groups, Jumano, Comecrudo, Tlaxcaltecas, Cherokee, and Lipan Apache, along with the Spanish, Italian, and many other Europeans who found their way to these lands. I acknowledge and ask permission of our ancestors to do "work that matters" as I write about these cultural expressions.

I acknowledge and thank Laredoans, especially the many collaborators whose *pláticas* over meals and in their homes fueled the work in this book. To the members of the Matachines de la Santa Cruz, especially the Ortiz family and Teresita González, who have honored me with their friendship and have over the years provided insight and shared their devotion to the Santa Cruz, ¡*Gracias*! I thank Laredoans who celebrate George Washington's birthday in all its complexity, including Candy Hein, Elaine Peña, Cordelia Barrera, the Botello family, and many others. I also have been honored to have been invited to numerous quinceañera celebrations hosted by my family and friends, as well as friends of friends; I was honored to have been invited to participate as a *madrina*, or a guest, in some of these celebrations. ¡Gracias!

To those who trusted me with their photographs: The Webb County Heritage Society and Jennifer Cantú for doing the research in their archives so we could find the historical images of the George Washington's Birthday Celebration, and Cristina Ibarra for allowing me to use stills from her documentary, *Las Martas*; to my grandniece Ariana Botello, thank you for allowing me to participate in your celebration and for the use of the photos; to Javier Ortiz's daughter, Norma Oralia Ortiz, for the use of her photographs of the Matachines de la Santa Cruz; Roxy Rios, for her assistance and for sharing her Pocahontas photo; to Sara Gonzalez Rendón, Margarita Martínez, and Maribel H. Portillo for facilitating the use of quinceañera photographs and especially the Rendón, Needham, and Melendez families for sharing the photos of their daughters' quinceañeras. To all who have welcomed me and answered my incessant questions with patience and genuine kindness over the years as I have studied these fiestas that are so close to my heart, ¡Gracias!

To those at UNT Press and at the Texas Folklore Society, especially Kristina Downs, my deepest appreciation and gratitude for the care and attention to the details and for all your efforts to make this book what it is. ¡Gracias!

Closer to home, mil gracias to Elsa and Elvia and others in my inner circle whose support makes my work possible ¡Gracias! Finally, as always, to the Creator and to all who guide my work on this and other realms, ¡Gracias!

Introduction

Finding Folklore, Fiestas, and Familia in Laredo, Texas

*Personal experiences—revised and in other ways redrawn—
become a lens with which to reread and rewrite the cultural
stories into which we are born.*
—Gloria Anzaldúa, "now let us shift . . ." (2002)

For some time now, I have been mulling the idea of a book that would weave my personal engagement with the three celebrations in Laredo, Texas, that comprise the heart of this book with ideas of a sentipensante folkloristics that I have been developing. When Kristina Downs asked me if I had anything on Texas folklore that I would consider submitting for publication by the Texas Folklore Society (TFS), I felt that I could not refuse such an opportunity to return to the TFS publications. After all, my first folklore publication was in one such volume—*Hecho en Tejas: Texas-Mexican Folk Arts and Crafts* (1991)—edited by Joe S. Graham, indomitable teacher and folklorist who taught folklore and anthropology at Texas A&M University-Kingsville. In that volume I had the honor of publishing with my students on the traditional practices of my beloved South

Texas. After following a rather unique trajectory both in my personal and professional life; after writing fiction, poetry, and scholarly literary criticism; after delivering and publishing academic papers; and after teaching about some of these celebrations, I feel I am ready to write about the particular celebratory events of my community that shaped who I am. Perhaps only now am I ready to critically scrutinize and think about the meaning of these festivals to my life and to the life of my community.

Fiestas in Laredo gathers my musings and scholarly take on three celebrations found in my hometown of Laredo, Texas: matachines, quinceañeras, and the George Washington's Birthday Celebration (GWBC). Anyone from Laredo will easily identify the particular flair these fiestas exhibit by just existing in the borderlands. To be sure, many more celebrations occur in our community; all are worthy of study. Among these are the usual Catholic liturgical celebrations such as Easter, Christmas, and Lent, and the secular celebrations that happen within the family circle, including birthdays with their use of piñatas, wedding and anniversary celebrations, bridal and baby showers, and even the burial rituals and commemorative celebrations like Veterans Day. By focusing on three areas of research that I have engaged in for the last forty years, *Fiestas in Laredo* sheds light on community practices and offers a peek into the traditions and contested spaces that often provide a counternarrative to the settler colonialism that the fiestas signify. Moreover, the official narrative that enshrines the celebrations sometimes obfuscates the "hidden transcripts," as James C. Scott (1992) would call the strategies that undergird unofficial resistance. In this case it is the celebrations, such as the Jalapeño Festival that is part of the GWBC or the matachines dance troupes that exist outside of the liturgical calendar.

But before I go into the fiestas themselves or into the theoretical considerations that I will be using—concepts developed by Chicana queer scholar Gloria E. Anzaldúa and the ideas derived from a sentipensante approach—it may help to offer a sort of self-disclosure statement that explains my interest in and my preparation for daring to enter into such a space, a space predicated on an insider perspective privileged by lived experience and embodied knowledge, a space that, as in most of my work, defies genre limitations. As Clifford Geertz ([1973] 2017) claimed about his own work, I am a writer who writes about culture, my own piece of the world. Whether in poetry, fiction, or academic writing, ultimately my writing remains solidly anchored in cultural expressions. As introduction I offer what Gloria Anzaldúa (2002, 578) would call *autohistoria,* a term she coins to "describe the genre of writing about one's personal and collective history using fictive elements, a sort of fictionalized autobiography or memoir; an autohistoria-teoría is a personal essay that theorizes."[1] In a sense it is my use of creative autobioethnography that I offer as a trellis upon which the rest of the chapters are attached.

My Travels along the Folklore Path

My path to folklore studies has been as nontraditional as can be. It has been a long one, and my travels along the path had many twists and turns. I first heard of the TFS when I was a first-generation, nontraditional undergraduate student at Texas A&I University at Laredo, now Texas A&M International University. I was working full time at a utilities company and studying for a degree in education with a double major in English and political science when my mentor, Dr. F. Allen Briggs, invited me to a meeting that was being held at the La Posada Hotel in Laredo sometime in the early 1970s. As a research assistant I later worked with Dr. Briggs and Dr. Alfredo Supervielle, translating and collating the items of children's folklore that the duo had collected from their students. Subsequently, during my MA program, I studied under Dr. Orlan Sawey at Texas A&I University-Kingsville, now Texas A&M University-Kingsville. I gave my first academic presentation at the TFS meeting held there; in fact, it was a paper I coauthored with Dr. Briggs.

But my interest in the fiestas, although grounded in my own lived experiences with the secular and religious folk celebrations in Laredo, began to solidify when I was looking for a topic for my doctoral dissertation. In 1975, home for the Christmas holidays from graduate school in Lincoln, Nebraska, I unwittingly—and, in retrospect, seren-dipitously—stumbled upon a *pastorela*, a Christmas shepherds' play, being performed on the grounds of the Laredo Public Library that was then housed in a building on Bruni Plaza. Intrigued by the performance and quite possibly because I was in search of a topic for a paper for a class, I immediately decided that I wanted to further explore the folk drama unfolding before me that warm South Texas Sunday afternoon. Thanks to the assistance of the librarian at the Laredo Public Library, Don Luciano Guajardo, *que en paz descanse* (RIP)—and with the encouragement of Dr. Briggs—I was able to connect with the group from Nuevo Laredo who performed the shepherds' play and to photo-copy a handwritten text kept in an old ledger.[2] Thus began my serious interest in the folk traditions that were part of my life in the border-lands where I lived—between Texas and Tamaulipas—particularly in the twin border cities of Laredo and Nuevo Laredo. Although I had been a participant and observer of the traditions for most of my life, and had been mildly interested in studying them, as an English major I had assumed that I would have to look at published works for my dissertation; in fact, my professors seemed to assume the same thing. So it took some convincing, but I was able to persuade my committee to accept my project and delve into the origins and significance of the folk play performed by a community group in their own home space, written in an old ledger, and kept by a family in Nuevo Laredo.

Although I had collaborated on a children's folklore collection as an undergraduate, I had little academic interest in the rich lore and traditions of my community. My dismissal of these as worthy topics of study can easily be attributed to the internalized racism and the effective socialization and cultural myopia of my public education at all levels in the decades of the fifties and sixties in public schools of South Texas.[3] The many overt and covert messages included physi-cal punishment for speaking Spanish in school. I learned the lessons well. By high school I had successfully separated my private world of pastorelas and matachines from my public world of record hops and rock and roll. And after high school, working as a clerk in the local utility company, as mentioned earlier, I continued to disassociate my private world of home and the public world of the office with more difficulty, for at the office I often encountered connections to my private world in the person of coworkers, especially one older office clerk, Vicente (RIP), who filled my head with stories of how "it used to be." He would tell of the folk tradition of *mojigangas* and the various plays he witnessed growing up in Laredo. I loved listening to his stories. In the varied positions I held at the office, I invariably had to deal with numerous customers both from Laredo and from the outside world, strangers to town. From the inside world of Laredo where we all knew each other's families, I observed what an intricate network of kinship and *compadrazgo* we shared; from those coming from the outside world, I learned that we were a curiosity, and that often they looked askance at our cultural expressions and judged us harshly for spending so much on a quinceañera or for celebrating George Washington's birthday. I was intrigued by it all and wondered whether I would ever achieve my dream of getting a college degree. In due time a branch of Texas A&I University opened up at the site of Laredo Junior College—now Laredo College—and I was able to finish my undergraduate degree. I was fortunate to meet professors who had an interest in folklore. That children's folklore collection that Professors Supervielle and Briggs prepared and for which I was a student assistant was my first foray into collecting.

At the time when I was a student of Dr. Briggs, the Texas Folklore Society met at La Posada in the historic downtown. He asked me to help with the registration and invited me to attend the conference. I did but paid little attention to the presentations; it all seemed so foreign to me as most of the participants and their topics of fiddling or of folklorists like J. Frank Dobie didn't interest me. I subsequently earned my master's degree in English from Texas A&I University and left to pursue a PhD at the University of Nebraska–Lincoln (UNL), away from South Texas, away from the known and to the unknown, away from my home and to the alien world of academia, away from the borderlands to the foreign world of Anglo Middle America.

In Nebraska I was further distanced from the traditions that had shaped my aesthetics, my very being. Luckily, I found family in Lincoln—distant cousins who had settled out of the migrant stream (and community, *raza*)—who in that cold alien place kept our traditions alive. I remember the excitement of listening to Sr. Reyes singing *corridos* and traditional songs, belting out el "Corrido del Caballo Blanco" or a favorite, "Los Laureles." The local Movimiento Estudiantil Chicano de Aztlán (MECHA) organization had a *folklórico* dance group that performed at local events. I loved to attend the monthly Mexican dances, where Tejano groups played to packed halls, reminding me of home. I saw many Tejano groups like Bernardo y sus Compadres and Little Joe y la Familia that toured the Midwest playing the working-class music from home. I yearned for the regional foods (cabrito, enchiladas), the herbal teas (manzanilla, canela), and the mariachi, Tejano, and conjunto music of the border. My graduate seminars on medieval literature, twentieth-century poetry, or the Romantic period in British Literature did not allow for explorations of folklore. Although Professors Elaine Jahner (RIP), Roger Welsch, and Paul Olson were teaching classes that did deal with what I would call folklore or cultural studies, I did not see a connection between what I was studying and who I was.

At that time, as an English major more inclined to reading Victorian novelists and a few Latin American writers—Carlos Fuentes, Pablo Neruda, and the other sixties and seventies heroes of Latin American letters—I did not fathom working on the "literature" of my own community. I was also piqued by my first forays into critical theory and seduced by the enterprise. Right before leaving Kingsville, where I had earned a master's degree in English, my American literature professor at Texas A&I, Cynthia Davis, passed on her Northrop Frye (1957) *Anatomy of Criticism*, saying something like, "You might be interested in this since you seem to like to think about such things." Indeed, I did. I devoured the book, understanding precious little I am sure, but smitten by the ideas. As I began work on my dissertation in the late seventies, I would only encounter a rare course in literary criticism. As I continued my studies at the University of Nebraska, Paul Olson and others provided guidance, but it was in Prof. Bruce Erlich's seminar where I first read other theorists and went beyond to Sigmund Freud, Karl Marx, and, yes, Ferdinand De Saussure and Claude Levi-Strauss—and eventually, after graduate school, Clifford Geertz, Frederic Jameson, and Mikhail Bakhtin—to look at connections between culture and literary production.

Initially, I had arrived at the nineteenth century, and specifically its women novelists, as a topic for my dissertation. But I was reading Antonio Gramsci (*Selections from the Prison Notebooks*, 1973), Franz Fanon (*Black Skin, White Masks*, 1967), and what were then, for me, the emerging feminist thinkers, Shulasmith Firestone (*The Dialectic of Sex: The Case for Feminist Revolution*, 1970), Simone de Beauvoir (*The Second Sex*, 1953), and Adrienne Rich (*On Lies, Secrets, and Silence: Selected Prose: 1966–1978*, 1979). At UNL I had long conversations with Elaine Jahner (RIP), a folklorist trained at Indiana University, and Hortense Spillers, an African American literary scholar, as well as with my dissertation directors, Ralph Grajeda (RIP) and Paul Olson. I had discussions with linguist Julia Stanley (RIP), who changed her name to Julia Penelope as a feminist act, and Moira Ferguson; both were immersed in feminist projects and building Women's Studies at UNL. From all of them I gleaned a sense of what a scholarly life could be, and I knew I had made the right decision. I remember clearly visiting Prof. Spillers at her home and being awed by the red walls of her study. I especially felt that I had embarked on the right path when I met one of my student's mothers, Beatriz George, a single mother and a local activist. With her and other women, we would visit the federal prison and provide translation services to the incarcerated. In some way the engagement with the community reinforced that the academic path was for me.

I soon realized that I wanted to work on something closer to home. I chose the pastorela, to the possible chagrin of my professors; Rafael

Francisco Grajeda (1974) had written one of the first dissertations on the Chicano novel, and I suspect he expected me to follow suit and work on a literary topic such as Chicano poetry. To his credit he was always supportive and nonjudgmental. I almost opted to switch to that more conventional (for an English department) route and look at the emerging Chicana writers that I was reading, especially the poets Bernice Zamora (*Restless Serpents*, 1976), Angela de Hoyos (*Chicano Poems: For the Barrio*, 1977), Inés Hernández Tovar (*Con Razón Corazón*, 1978), Evangelina Vigil-Piñón (*Nade y Nade*, 1978), and Lorna Dee Cervantes (*Emplumada*, 1981).

As fate would have it, the pastorela manuscript became my topic instead of either the nineteenth-century novel or Chicano/a/x literature. In 1979–1980, all course work completed, and thanks to a Fulbright-Hays research grant, I spent an academic year in Madrid researching the origins and developments of the pastorela. I somehow saw myself as following in the footsteps of other Chicana folklorists like Jovita González (*Folk-lore of the Texas-Mexican Vaquero*, 1927), Aurora Lucero-White Lea (*Literary Folklore of the Hispanic Southwest*, 1953) and Cleofas Jaramillo (*Shadows of the Past*, 1972), whose work I had begun to read and admire. I felt I had found my literary foremothers, as it were, and yearned to not merely document but also—armed with tools—analyze the material that they had merely collected and which I naïvely thought was fast disappearing.

My semiotic analysis of the shepherds' play was going in a direction no one in the department quite understood, but they were willing to let me pursue it. As critical and as transformative as my work on the pastorela was, it was the work that I began *after* I returned to Laredo to teach at my alma mater, which was by then called Laredo State University, that led me to folklore and the study of the traditional culture of my community. I began researching the matachines dance tradition in the mid-1980s as I collaborated with folklorists who were researching the tradition for what was then the American Folklife Festival, organized by the Smithsonian Institution. One of the main programs for the 1987 festival was called *America's Many Languages*; Frank Proschan was the main curator. The experience was transformative on many levels, as it was then that I met people who would become lifelong friends, like Dan Sheehy, Olivia Cadaval, and Alicia González. I returned to Laredo after the festival with the intention of writing a book on the matachines. Not surprisingly, I began researching other traditional cultural expressions such as the quinceañeras that my nieces were celebrating and began to also look at the community's premier festival, the GWBC, with a critical eye. In 1993 I went to work at the National Endowment for the Arts (NEA) Folk and Traditional Arts Program through an Intergovernmental Personnel Act position that allowed me to leave my university position in Laredo and move to Washington, DC, for the job. I was fortunate to then meet Bess Lomax Hawes and work with Terry Liu and Barry Bergey. Through my work at the NEA, I met many public folklorists and established a strong personal network that spanned that aspect of folklore work that I had only been made aware of marginally because in the 1980s I had secured an apprenticeship through Texas Folklife Resources. The apprenticeship allowed me to relearn how to construct the traditional single piece quilts we call *colchas* from an elder in San Ygnacio, Texas, Doña María Solis; my grandmother used to make them, so my mother was thrilled that I was recovering that family tradition. I was immersed in folklife studies but still not calling myself a folklorist; basically, I felt that if I had not earned a PhD in the discipline, I was an imposter.

Finally, I want to highlight my pedagogical work in the field. After I returned to my teaching position as an English professor, I became more and more active in the American Folklore Society, and I began inserting folklore into my classes. Later, when I left Laredo and joined the faculty at the University of Texas San Antonio, I taught a study abroad summer class in Spain titled "The Spanish Roots of Chicana/o Folklore." For eight years I took groups of students for three-week sessions at the Universidad de Castilla–La Mancha. I conducted daily classes, and we visited a number of sites and folk artists; we always scheduled the class to coincide with Toledo's Corpus Christi celebration so we also had ample access to secular and religious festivals. All along I had been attending the matachines celebrations in Laredo and of course attending quinceañeras and the GWBCs. I presented my work at the American Studies Association, the National Association for Chicana and Chicano Studies, and the American Folklore Society (AFS) annual meetings and at various other venues as an invited speaker; I published articles here and there and at some point, especially as I lectured on the topic, I started thinking about writing a book.

This book is an attempt to bring my thinking and writing about these three celebrations to an audience beyond my students. Furthermore, I try out a new concept that I have been playing with for a while. The folkloristics of the twenty-first century cannot remain the same as that of previous centuries. Our position is no different from that of the folklorists in the late twentieth century who moved forward beyond the nineteenth century's practice of collecting to analysis and theoretical constructs to explain social phenomena and seek answers to the conundrum that is the human condition; we are on the threshold of a new and exciting phase of what our field can be and do. In my presidential address at the AFS annual meeting in Harrisburg, Pennsylvania, in 2021, I introduced a way of thinking about our work, a sentipensante folkloristics. I now bring this concept into conversation here as I braid my own personal narrative and the three fiestas that are the subject of this book. Briefly, the core belief behind the idea of sentipensante is the unity or holistic view of humankind as one totalizing organism that both thinks and feels at once. Unlike much of nineteenth- and twentieth-century thought, with its reliance on the rational and its denial of the affective, of our feelings—for the twenty-first century what was old is new again as we retrieve modes of thinking from what has existed in the Global South for thousands of years. A sentipensante folkloristics, much like a sentipensante pedagogy, as articulated by Laura Rendón (2014), seeks to consider the whole human being, with both feeling and thinking having equal weight, and not privilege the thinking over the feeling.

Our world has changed and we must change with it, as became obvious with the response globally to the COVID-19 pandemic. To survive fiestas too must adapt and change, and the Laredo celebrations are no exception. The three celebrations at the center of this book coexist in my hometown of Laredo, Texas, a site that itself is historic and rooted in folk traditions. My brief analysis of the fiestas includes some commentary beyond the collecting and the purely descriptive. Perhaps by writing this short book on these three fiestas that occur in the context of a border that—as Chicana philosopher Anzaldúa ([1987] 2019) explained—is an "open wound," I can encourage others to build upon and theorize around the cultural production of marginalized nonmigrant and migrant communities in the United States, communities that have resisted settler colonialism with culture-affirming expressions. Laredo is at the interstices of cultures, of politics, of lives lived along the margins.

My childhood memories tell me that I have been aware of these celebrations almost from infancy. I am about three when I hold on tight to my dad's hand as the Viejo comes after me at a matachines dance at Mother Cabrini Church. I am terrified. The second memory is less scary but also lingers in my mind. We are at my Tía Inés's backyard. The relationship is complicated. Inés was Tío Gonzalo's wife in the United States; he had another wife in Monterrey, Mexico, but I am no more than five, so I don't know these things and my uncle has been dead some ten years, having been killed in a barroom fight in a small town in Northern Mexico, supposedly an instance of mistaken identity. It's his daughter, my cousin Ramona's, quinceañera. My parents are dancing to boleros coming from a record player. I am the oldest so I hold on to my brother's hand and watch over my baby sister, Laura, while our parents dance round and round the dance floor; my mother waves each time they glide by. I enjoy the food and marvel at how my cousin was transformed into an angelic apparition—her poofy dress, the sparkly diadem on her head. She was beautiful! The third memory is one of hundreds of GWBC memories. I am on my dad's shoulders and so I can see the parade and marvel at all that comes before me—including military tanks; it is only four years since the end of World War II, after all. A few years later, I am dressed as a *china poblana*, the traditional dress that most signifies Mexicanness, to go to the parade, and a few years after that my friends and I go to the carnival and flirt with the guys from Mexico and ride the Ferris wheel and eat cotton candy. So many memories!

In this book I weave some of these memories (the warp) with research and *pláticas* (the weft)[4] to render a sentipensante Anzaldúan analysis. Additionally, in this manuscript I discuss the approaches to the study of *transfronteriza*, or cross-border cultural expressions, specifically the fiestas as they play out uniquely in the rich cultural context that is the border, that space that is unique in its cultural expressions. The customs, the fiestas, and the folkways of a people that have layers upon layers of cultural identifiers—from the Indigenous to the Spanish to the Mexican and the United Statesian, all rooted in a *tejanidad*, a regional identity that blends all of them—all reveal many of the complexities of a borderlands *transfronteriza* cultural milieu. As a child growing up in Laredo, these celebrations were integral to my life formation. The religious expression rooted in a folk Catholic tradition that goes back to the confluence of faith-based dance tradition, and the cousin's or neighbor's quinceañeras and, later as a teen, my friends' and my own celebration, filled me with excitement.

Unlike the fiestas of rural Mexico or even of Texas, the fiestas in the borderlands exhibit the hybridity of the confluence that exists as two nations edge each other out along what Anzaldúa ([1987] 2019) called the "open wound" that will not heal, the border. The scholar of Mexican folklore Stanley Brandes (1988) notes that rural Mexican fiestas paradoxically "promote order and social control, although they seem to provide a break from ordinary routine and can even appear formless and chaotic . . . fiestas provide respites from the constraints and rules of everyday life" (1–2). I have observed the same of the fiestas in rural Spain. Similarly, the fiestas in Laredo promote a form of order and social control while providing "a break from ordinary routine" even as the annual matachines and GWBCs establish a grammatical order of sorts where the social stratification is reified and maintained from generation to generation.

I now turn to defining terms I use in talking about the fiestas; specifically, I ferret out the main elements that help in an analysis of these cultural expressions.

Definitions

The definition of terms such as *festival* and *fiesta* are geographically and situationally located. What for some is a fiesta, others may call a festival, and vice versa. After discussion of the terms *ritual*, *festival*, and *fiesta*, Brandes (1988) concludes that "fiestas . . . are literally feasts, shared events that people plan for and participate in jointly." He adds, "They usually assume a traditional form—or at least are perceived by the participants to do so—and they generally are invested with sacred significance" (9). Just as in previous eras in Laredo, the term *fiesta* was usually associated almost exclusively with a saint's day celebration and rarely referred to a secular event; now it has widened in meaning to refer to any feast or celebration. One may hear *Andamos de fiesta* to mean "We are partying" just as often as *La fiesta es mañana* to mean "The party is tomorrow" or "The festival is tomorrow." The scholarly distinctions of what constitutes a feast, a fiesta, or a festival do not necessarily exist for this community. In Laredo the word *fiesta* applies for all three; people refer to *la fiesta de matachines, la fiesta de quinceañera,* and *la fiesta de George Washington* (on Mexican radio it is referred to as *la fiesta de Jorge Washington*). Discussing the definitions of what we call the festive events, I am drawn to the work of folklorist Beverly J. Stoeltje, whose work helped me understand the principal components of festival studies. From her studies of rodeos and of beauty pageants, along with her critical work on defining the term *festival*, I arrive at the essential elements that comprise a

festival—but are they the same for fiestas? or feasts? According to
Stoeltje (1992), a festival is public and includes elements of participant engagement. The events are "complex in structure, and multiple
in voice, scene, and purpose" (261). She notes that the event serves
a collective need and that it is the social group that is at the center of
the event. She further notes that its continuity is ensured via systems
of reciprocity, whereby participants exchange labor or goods. Moreover, the sense of shared responsibility—in a way the allocation of
prestige and production—further cements the bonds among participants and guarantees the passing on of the tradition (261). While
Brandes studies the fiesta as social control, using the fiesta as a lens
that reveals a community's power and persuasion, Stoeltje sees these
events as more than performative expressions.

As I've discussed elsewhere (Cantú 2010), secular and religious
celebrations often intersect, and it is common to have a secular festival coincide with a saint's feast day. Such fusion results in multilay-
ered festival events; thus the fiesta or festival is a hybrid and exists
in what Anzaldúa (1987, 276) called "nepantla"—a space that allows
for both the secular and the religious to coexist simultaneously and
allows for individuals within a community to select what aspect of the
event best suits them. The liturgical cyclical celebrations are a case
in point. For instance, at Christmas folks may observe the event by
focusing on gift giving or the family meal or the social aspects of
posadas and not attend religious services or church-sponsored events.
Curiously, figures such as Santa Claus embody both the secular and
religious; the Papá Noel Vasco, Olentzero, the Basque equivalent
("Nor Gara" 2020), functions in a similar fashion, bringing gifts at
Christmas, but has roots in pre-Christian winter solstice celebrations.
Traditions like the Christmas tree or the *ramo de Navidad Leones* in
Spain signal a region's allegiance to what are evidently nonliturgical
elements.[5] Similarly, someone attending the matachines celebration
may do so out of custom, or as an occasion to visit family and socially
engage with the community; they may not necessarily see it as a religious event, often eschewing attending mass or offering any personal

prayers. The reason for and meaning of the event, then, is not singular but polysemic in that the same event may signify different things for different participants or members of the community; however, at the core of the event are the consequences of its existence. The collective or metafestive meaning functions as an umbrella under which various secular or liturgical subsets coexist. In all three of the fiestas that are the object of study in this book, people come together for a collective undertaking, a community's bonds are strengthened, and the group's identity is affirmed.

Rites, rituals, and spectacles may also happen for similar reasons: to bring the community together for a collective event. Rites are often focused on the individual. So it is for religious rites of passage like the sacraments for Catholics (such as baptism, confirmation, communion, wedding), or secular rites of passage like the quinceañera or high school prom; rituals, on the other hand, are most often associated with religious practice and involve a performance—collective or individual—of a repeated act not necessarily performed by the participant (Rappaport 1992, 249). For our purposes, rituals, rites, and festivals are unique and separate, although they may at times intersect, as in the matachines. On the other hand, as Manning (1992) has noted, spectacles occur on a large scale and involve a cultural production with various moving parts grouped around a specific focus. Thus, the GWBC can be classified as spectacle, the matachines as ritual, and the quinceañera as rite. But all are referred to as fiestas in the local lexicon. Hence, I use the term *fiesta* in the title of the book; moreover, I want to emphasize that the term *fiesta* as used in the community of Laredo is generic and is used to refer to all three events and similar celebratory communal events.

Another key term that I use extensively is *Borderlands* with a capital *B* to distinguish this Anzaldúan construct or theoretical approach from the term *borderlands*, lower case *b*, that refers to the geographical region. The fact that these fiestas occur along the borderlands allows for a particular analysis of *transfronteriza* aesthetics and cultural expressions. A Borderlands analysis further explores the connection of the cultural context that places the events in a space that is at once conflictive and confluent; that is, while the event may exist along a real, physical borderlands, it allows for a theorizing of its elements as either in opposition to or in agreement with the other.

Theories and Approaches

Scholars who have looked at festivals invariably study the ways that such events showcase a community's identity and how the community transmits values through the festival. Theorizing from a sociological or anthropological perspective, scholars have looked at festivals as events whose existence depends on the community even as the community is ultimately why they exist. Using my usual autobioethnograpy as a genre to explore the cultural production, I integrate images, memory, scholarship, and a collaborative research practice as I construct this manuscript. Drawing from my work with Gloria Anzaldúa's concepts and engaging with a discussion of sentipensante folkloristics to discern the ways these fiestas allow for resistance to the settler colonial logics of a borderlands space, I argue we can glean a better and more informed view of the Borderlands ethos of Laredo. I am working with the ideas that address what María Lugones (2010) called the "enmeshments," as opposed to the intersectionality of oppressive structures, and thus lay out a narrative that underscores the many layered social and cultural conditions. I want to go beyond what Kimberlé Crenshaw (1989) articulated constitutes intersectionality to what Anzaldúa ([1987] 2019) had previously pointed out, albeit without coining a phrase or word, to refer to the ways social structures deploy class, race, ability, age, gender, sexuality, and other conditions for discrimination and oppression, collapsing these multiple identifiers at the center of an axis of oppressions. My own theories and methods of analysis draw from Anzaldúa and Lugones, as much as on the folklorists, anthropologists, and ethnographers who have come before.

Chapter Summaries

Chapter 1 begins with an analysis of the folk Catholic dance tradition of the matachines, as its appearance in the community more than likely precedes the other two chronologically. I explore how this tradition has survived and the aspects of folk Catholicism that are involved in the tradition. What intrigues me is how the dance troupe seems to hold on to the tradition despite the onslaught of influences that would have them disband and erase the cultural expressions: folk belief, along with elements of material culture including dress, the wooden cross, and foodways. In my other work on the matachines, I delve into the fiesta in much more detail, but for purposes of this book, I limit the chapter to a discussion of the way the community of matachín dancers constitutes a layer of Laredo social strata that is not always recognized and yet also overlaps with other traditions such as Christmas rituals. From a sentipensante perspective, the matachines embody the thinking and feeling aspect, an embodiment of the physical and spiritual. It is an embodied prayer through dance. The physical body holds the affective and spiritual meaning for the celebration.

In Chapter 2 I turn to the quinceañera tradition and how I see it institutionalizing both a kind of kinship relationship that creates community and a performance of culture and identity within a secular and semireligious event. I began interviewing and collecting data on the tradition in the early 1990s as my nieces began having quinceañeras, although, to be frank, I probably began questioning and thinking about the celebration when I celebrated my own fiesta in 1962. I explore the intricate network of what I would call an approach to making *familia*, not from scratch necessarily, but certainly from the elements that form community.[6] My interest is more aligned with a feminist analysis of the tradition, and I explore the tradition as an expression that confronts late capitalism with the ways young women become acculturated into what is the feminine and then look at how these same young women disrupt the master narrative that is how their families and society see the often criticized event—criticized by outsiders because of the expense and because the families will often go into debt to cover the cost of the celebration. The sentipensante aspect of quinceañeras becomes obvious as the celebration has morphed into a twenty-first-century performance of not just social coming of age but of spiritual and political identity, an integration of the thinking and feeling aspects.

In Chapter 3 I address the ways that the GWBC brings together various sectors of society in a secular celebration. Also, from a personal perspective, I incorporate the work of fellow Laredoans Elaine A. Peña and Cordelia F. Barrera and their recent books, ¡Viva George! Celebrating Washington's Birthday at the US-Mexico Border (2020) and The Haunted Southwest: Towards an Ethics of Place in Borderlands Literature (2022), respectively. Peña explores the political aspects of the celebration, ensconced as it is within the fabric of Laredo society, while Barrera positions the celebration at the crux of her analysis of the land, the borderlands, and the literature. Both scholars use their own engagement with the celebration to present theoretical analyses. From a sentipensante folkloristics lens, I would say that the celebration elicits feelings and thoughts, complex and sometimes contradictory, of how and why Laredo would host such a celebration.

Drawing from personal experience and definitely braiding the narrative with my personal recollections of all these three fiestas, I answer some basic questions around notions of citizenship, social justice, and belonging, all the while exploring the ways that these fiestas form social bonds in the community and create intricate lazos de comprensión, bonds of understanding, that defy the forces that would eradicate or at least change them. By "forces" I mean the layers of colonialism from the earliest days of Spanish incursions into the region and culminating in the push for acculturation wrought through the push for modernity and to the postmodern scenario of dystopic dimensions.

Throughout the analysis and discussion of these three celebrations, I use what Ruth Behar (1996) would identify as a "heart-bound analysis"—what I consider another manifestation of sentipensante approach—using my own experiences and my engagement with the traditions during my lifetime as a resident of Laredo and the border.[7] Furthermore, since I am laying out a lens for doing folklore study from a sentipensante folkloristics, and following Anzaldúa's charge that we use theories and approaches imagined by us to work through the intricacies of our own cultural and material expressions, I put forth a theory of how cultural expressions can be studied and what information they can offer both the outsiders and the participants themselves. As I mentioned above, these fiestas build a social bond while also contesting existing structures; for instance, the quinceañera performances that are staged as political events signal a shift from the ways the celebration existed in the past. I borrow from Rendón's (2014) *Sentipensante Pedagogy*, a theoretical approach based on the concept that originates in the Caribbean coast of Colombia with the Indigenous groups that follow a more integrative way of life that doesn't separate the feeling from the thinking. The conceptual engagement is bound to the affective in essential ways. My own analysis is a thinking/feeling process of integrating scholarly and life writing.

As a book about fiestas, the celebratory tone underscores the sentiment that a fiesta brings. Like the celebration of a birthday signals passage of time, so thus these celebrations mark transitions and timely rituals. What van Gennep (1960) termed "rites of passage" I see as transitions along a trajectory that has led me to this very book where I reflect on the fiestas, the celebrations, the life markers that may offer a way into a world, a portal of sorts to the borderlands and the expressive culture of a world that lies at the interstices, in nepantla where people exist along a world that is often at odds and yet remains coherent in part due to these celebrations.

Chapter 1

Soldiers of the Holy Cross
Los Matachines de la Santa Cruz

Con o sin dinero, los matachines bailan.
—Sarita Liendo

Once a matachín, always a matachín.
—Florencio Ortiz

In May 2019 I walk onto the *terreno*, the city lot where the Matachines de la Santa Cruz gather to dance in honor of the Holy Cross in May and for the Virgen de Guadalupe's feast day on December 12. It's been a few years since I have attended the ceremony, so I am greeted warmly and welcomed into the circle of families, the community that gathers to dance and to watch the dancers. But most of all they gather because of their faith belief in the Holy Cross; they come to pray. Little did we know the fiesta would be put on pause as the COVID-19 pandemic would put everything on hold. Although the fiesta, prohibited by the city for safety reasons, didn't happen in May 2020 or 2021, the dancing occurred within the family. In 2021 I spoke to who may be considered the matriarch of the Ortiz clan, Doña Panchita Ortiz. She confirmed that there would not be a procession, a mass, or the dancing in the *terreno*. According to her this would be the first time that the matachines would not publicly celebrate the fiesta and dance for the Holy Cross. Trying to adhere to the city-imposed mandate prohibiting gatherings of more than ten people in 2020, the Ortiz brothers met and conducted the dance for a very private and limited audience—their own immediate family; they did the same in 2021, although by then the limit had been lifted but gatherings were still prohibited. The COVID restrictions were still in place, however, when the dance troupe received the National Heritage Fellowship from the National Endowment for the Arts (NEA) in 2021. In December they danced for the Virgen de Guadalupe, again with only immediate family participating. The Austin film crew that recorded it for the NEA drove right back to Austin after the filming. By May 2022 the dancing resumed and the fiesta happened. I was unable to attend, but from all accounts it was a joyful reunion and many danced to the Holy Cross in thanksgiving for having survived COVID.

Since 1938 the Matachines de la Santa Cruz have been dancing on the day of the Holy Cross, May 3, in a traditional folk Catholic fiesta that includes a procession, a dance, a festive meal, and prayers. The two rows of dancers wear a red vest and a *nagüilla* (a kind of skirt made of two flaps of heavy, red velvet with sequin embroidered figures and words, including the dancer's name) while holding a rattle and a stylized bow and arrow also used as a noisemaker in some of the *sones* (dance tunes). The recognition by the NEA came at a time of transition as the troupe is still strong and new leaders are emerging.

Although I completed a dissertation on the pastorela, the traditional shepherds' play, and went on to do further work in folklore, it is the matachines that have kept me enthralled and at work on a book for over forty years. I harbor a special place for the tradition that touched me as a child attending the fiesta at Mother Cabrini Church with my parents in the barrio Cantarranas. At that time in the early 1950s, the matachines groups were few and mostly derived from the group that had moved to Laredo in the 1930s. The group around Mother Cabrini Church and the one at Holy Redeemer had both moved to Laredo from Las Minas, and although separate, they were dancing to the same sones and to music provided by neighborhood members who played accordion, violin, guitar, and the basis of all matachines troupes: the drum. The structure of the fiesta was identical to what it is now: an opening, several sones, including specific footwork and choreographies, and a closing, or *despedida*, over a span of anywhere from three to five days.

As described in the introduction, the tradition exists across the Americas in variants that run the gamut from those entrenched in the Catholic Church to those that exist outside of any church affiliation at all. In all cases the dance tradition forms part of a complex cultural web while ostensibly existing in a community to honor and celebrate a particular feast day; most often it is associated with the Virgen de Guadalupe, or it may also exist to honor other saints such as San Lorenzo in Bernalillo, New Mexico. The cultural expressions and the faith belief that underpin it signify that it is part of a complex system of cultural expressions and beliefs.

One of my earliest memories, as I noted in the introduction, is of attending a matachines fiesta. I remember being comforted and subsequently healed *de susto* (of fright) because of a scare I took when as a child no more than three years old; the Viejo from the matachines frightened me. El Viejo, the protagonist of the son that bears his name, is a scarily clad matachín dancer who often brandishes a whip in one hand and a doll in the other and whose sole purpose is to distract the dancers and to scare the spectators. El Viejo is also found in the pastorela, the Christmas shepherds' play that is the subject of my dissertation, as a hermit who joins the shepherds on their way to honor the Christ child. I am led to another memory: my cousin Socorro—or Corito, as we lovingly called her—ten years my senior, takes me, an impressionable five-year-old, to a pastorela and matachines performances in Anáhuac, Nuevo León, a small town in Northern Mexico where my paternal grandparents had settled and where we visited often. I remember holding on to her hand in terror as I faced fire-breathing devils and el Viejo, the old man with a whip; nightmares haunted me for several nights after we returned to our home in Laredo. I don't recall a healing this time, though, as I knew it was part of the performance and probably didn't suffer the symptoms of *susto* as I had the first time.

During my dissertation research on the pastorela, I pursued a parallel current of investigation as I kept finding allusions to matachines performance and rituals in old manuscripts at the Biblioteca Nacional in Madrid. I returned to Spain in 1985 to further study festivals and celebrations in general, and once again in culling through the manuscripts in the *biblioteca*, I found manuscripts and references to matachines in Spanish tradition. By then I had begun to attend the annual celebration of a particular Laredo group, the Matachines de la Santa Cruz de la Ladrillera. In the summer of 1976, I had first interviewed a member of that group, Sarita Liendo, the grandmother of one of my brothers-in-law. From that first meeting, when I was still in graduate school and home for the summer, I had felt a connection. She made me feel comfortable talking with her. She welcomed me into her three-room *casita*, a wood-frame house painted the color of the sky at dusk, a musty blue. I had not had any formal training in interviewing techniques, as the tape of that interview reveals only too well, but I knew instinctively that I should audiotape my conversations and that the information—indeed the entire interaction—would be a significant part of my work in Laredo.

It has been almost fifty years since my first interview with Sarita Liendo, may she rest in peace, but I am convinced that it was on that first visit to her home that I embarked on my current work; this chapter is a part of a longer book-length project. I left her three-room frame house with a bag of dried chamomile for tea, another bag of basil seeds, and a head full of ideas for a book, a book that remains to be finished. I didn't know at the time that I was being led to write about a tradition that was crucial for the identity of a tightly knit community; I was still focused on other traditions like the pastorela. In many ways the matachines community has become my second family in Laredo. The passing of the brothers, the elders Pedro (Pete) Ortiz and Florencio (Palafox) Ortiz in 1993, provided the final impetus, for this project is a fulfillment of a vow to both of them and to Doña Sarita that I would write the story of the Santa Cruz, the Holy Cross, and the community that honors and venerates the holy icon. But I cannot tell the story of the matachines tradition in Laredo without telling the story of the individuals, the families, and the community where the Holy Cross resides and where I have spent so many hours. Nor can it be told without some reference to the larger community of Laredo, Texas, the languages we speak, the ways we worship, and the ways we celebrate. *La fiesta de matachines* constitutes a site of celebration that collapses both secular and religious realms.

In September of 1993, I went to sixty-seven-year-old Florencio Ortiz Jr.'s funeral. The image of our last visit but a couple of weeks earlier haunted me. Right after the service I drove to Washington, DC, where I was to begin working at the NEA Folk and Traditional Arts Program, while on leave from my teaching job at what was then Laredo State University, now Texas A&M International University. As I drove, a bright rainbow magically appeared in the horizon. It wasn't raining, and I took it as an omen that Mr. Ortiz was with me. I kept remembering his hearty laugh, his voice, his laughing green eyes. That night in Dallas where we stopped en route to DC, I dreamed the first of several dreams: I am looking for the fiesta, and finally I hear the familiar drum beat calling the dancers, and I follow the sound to a courtyard where the cross has been set up and people are gathering. Palafox welcomes me; "Creíamos que ya no venía" (We thought you weren't coming),[1] he says as he beats the drum and is attentive to the dancers at the same time as he speaks to me. For me dreams have invariably signaled change and often have offered information or messages that have shaped my life. In this case, I interpreted the dream to mean that the community thought I had abandoned them by leaving for DC. I woke up with a renewed sense of mission. I would write about the tradition and support it as long as I could in whatever way I could. In a way this chapter fulfills my promise, at least in part. When I finish the monograph on the *fiesta de matachines*, I will have fulfilled it totally.

In this chapter I describe the fiesta and situate it within the traditions that have elements from Indigenous rituals as well as European accouterments that render them true cultural *mestizaje*.[2] Further, I offer a few thoughts as to why the fiesta remains as a cultural expression after over a hundred years in the area, passed down by family members from one generation to the next. My aim is not to do a full analysis of the fiesta; that is what I will do in my book project on the Matachines de la Santa Cruz. Instead, I place my analysis within the scope of looking at the three fiestas that are the subject of this book. I seek to place the *fiesta de matachines* at the center of a discussion of how the region's Indigenous past is reinforced and affirmed. I situate the fiesta within the community's identity—an identity forged for over two centuries into one of contradictions in a complex cultural existence where Indigenous ways of being are all but gone, where settler colonialism persists, and where life continues despite the tremendous odds against survival.

History of the Tradition

In my research I have identified various dance traditions that are called matachines. Most prominent for South Texas and Northern Mexico are the matachines de la flecha. The matachines de la palma and matachines de la pluma are also danced in greater Mexico, but not to the same degree. The origins of the dance are contested, and each group has an origin story of how they came to the tradition. For instance, the group in Laredo that is the subject of this chapter honor the Holy Cross because the Holy Cross is miraculous; a few years ago, some of the elders recounted the legend of how Santa Elena went in search of the Holy Cross and rescued it from the infidels and how they came to possess it. At least one person told me that the cross they danced to was the true cross where Jesus was crucified, but that conversation of over thirty years ago situates the history in an imagined past. The elders I spoke to have passed away, and more recently I have asked the same question only to find that very few dancers even know the legend of Santa Elena and how she found the true cross that they venerate. Most will reference the move from the mining towns upriver and few even know that the group originated in Mexico.

Pre-European Origins

Coahuiltecan groups roamed the area of South Texas and Laredo because its position as a natural crossing was a favorite spot. In 1755 as part of the Escandón expedition, several families led by Don Tomás Sánchez settled in what is now Laredo, Texas, and Nuevo Laredo, Tamaulipas. The area had been inhabited by the Indigenous peoples that included mostly Coahuiltecan Carrizo groups and later included the Lipan Apache. In less than a century, the settlement grew and became an important point along the Camino Real going from Zacatecas to New Orleans. This passage is also called the Camino Real de los Tejas and can be traced to the route that spanned from Zacatecas to Los Adaes in Louisiana (De la Teja 1998). Some of the participants in the matachines have told me they inherited the tradition from the elders who brought it from Real de Catorce, a small mining community in the state of San Luis Potosi in Northern Mexico that was an important colonial municipality. While that would lead one to assume that the tradition's Indigenous roots would be Huichol, it appears more plausible that the Tlaxcaltecas who traveled with the Spanish to the northern states brought a similar dance celebration with them. Or perhaps it is the Tarahumara whose matachines are similar to the tradition in New Mexico. I saw a group of Tarahumara matachines at the American Folklife Festival in Washington, DC, whose rendition was similar to the tradition I saw in Bernalillo, New Mexico, yet had a very different "feel" as the elements were not as Eurocentric as the ones in Bernalillo, where the dance honors San Lorenzo. Scholars like Sylvia Rodríguez (1994, 1996, 2009) who have written about the tradition invariably decline to offer a definitive origin or to assign a definitive meaning to the danza. Adrian Treviño and Barbara Gilles (1994) emphasize the Indigenous origins while Cleofas M. Jaramillo (1972, 50) points to mixed Indigenous and European origins: "Some say that it is an Aztec dance; others believe it to be of Spanish and Moorish origin. My mother told me that it was the dance danced by the Aztecs when they went to meet Montezuma on his visits to the different pueblos. The writer feels the Spanish and Aztec blend most likely as evidenced by the names *Malinche* and *Monarca* [two characters who typically appear in matachines dance performances]. The name Matachines has been traced back to an Arabic word, meaning 'maskers,' suggesting that the dance drama was brought from across the sea." The particular group that is the subject of this chapter can definitively assert that their aboriginal dance was brought from Mexico, although it is not clear if it was a Mexican tradition.[3]

The New Mexico tradition is perhaps the most documented and studied; Sylvia Rodríguez (1994, 1996, 2009), Max Harris[4] (1994, 1997), and other scholars such as Brenda Romero (1993, 1997, 1999) have written extensively about the New Mexico tradition. Two books on the tradition in Texas, Robert Botello's *We Dance for the Virgen: Authenticity of Tradition in a San Antonio Matachines Troupe* (2022) and my own unpublished *Soldiers of the Cross: Los Matachines de la Santa Cruz* add to the scholarship on the tradition in Texas.

The dance tradition of the matachines exists throughout the Americas, dating back to the Spanish colonial period. In the twenty-first century, troupes of matachín dancers can be found throughout what Américo Paredes (1976, xiv) termed Greater Mexico, areas where Mexican-origin peoples live on both sides of the US-Mexico border. Whereas the matachines traditions that are now present in New Mexico, Texas, and elsewhere in the United States may have been more strictly bound to the official Catholic Church rituals during the colonial period, they now occupy spaces outside the liturgical or sanctioned church spaces. Many of the elders recall a time when outside of church sponsorship the group would perform not only during liturgical holidays like Christmas but also during local saints' days celebrations and always during the Virgen de Guadalupe feast day on December 12. Some scholars trace the tradition back to Indigenous dance worship even before the conquest in Mexico (Harris 2000, 18). Still, the tradition in what is now the Southwest of the United States seems to have autochthonous elements from Indigenous groups in the area and from farther south, such as the Tlaxcaltecas who accompanied the Spanish as they moved into northern territories and some elements from the Spanish, including the use of certain musical instruments such as the guitar or accordion.[5]

At least ten matachines groups have existed in Laredo for over twenty years, but the particular group that is the subject of this chapter, Los Matachines de la Santa Cruz de la Ladrillera, has been here since the 1930s, as I stated earlier (figs. 1.1, 1.2). They were previously situated in an area called Las Minas, upriver from Laredo.

Many still tell of how their grandparents or great-grandparents came from Mexico to work in the coal mines and then moved to Laredo. The group's trajectory—from a particular mining town in central Mexico, Real de Catorce, to the mining towns along the Rio Grande and finally to Laredo—leads to an analysis of displacement and of resettlement (Cantú 2012). Through oral tradition we know that the move from central Mexico into Northern Mexico and to what is now South Texas occurred due to the closing of the silver and gold mines in Real de Catorce sometime in the late nineteenth and early twentieth centuries. We also know that the Tlaxcaltecan influence can be traced to that area and that it became more pronounced along the way. As the silver mines were closed, the miners migrated with the mining company to the coal mines of South Texas, settling in several small towns—Santo Tomás, Palafox, Minera, Canel, and Dolores—collectively known as Las Minas (García, n.d.). They brought the Matachines dance tradition and the faith belief in the Holy Cross with them. When the coal mines closed in the 1930s, the families moved to Laredo and found jobs at a brick factory; they settled in the neighborhood around the brick factory, La Ladrillera.[6]

Fig. 1.1 The Matachines de la Santa Cruz de la Ladrillera. Children making their first communion were part of the celebration up until the mid-1960s. Photo courtesy of the Ortiz family.

Fig. 1.2 The Matachines de la Santa Cruz de la Ladrillera troupe posed for a group photo in 1942. At the time only men and boys were allowed to dance. Photo courtesy of the Ortiz family.

Fig. 1.3 Led by Capitanes Rey and Javier Ortiz, the Matachines de la Santa Cruz de la Ladrillera dance in procession from the *terreno* to Holy Redeemer Church. Community members guide the cross and follow behind the dancers, praying. 2018. Photo by Norma Oralia Ortiz.

Until the 1930s only adult men and teenage boys danced; no children were allowed to participate. But by the post–World War II era, younger boys were dancing alongside the elders. After some resistance, women began dancing in the late 1960s. Nowadays, this traditional folk-Catholic dance has become intergenerational as they invite dancers of all ages and is inclusive of dancers from as young as five to as old as eighty, although the latter is a rarity, no doubt due to the physical challenge the dancing demands. Such range allows the young members to learn from the elders; however, in the past twenty years, I have observed fewer and fewer elders dancing as those who once were the *capitanes* (captains), or the leaders, of the dance age and take on other roles in the Matachines community and new capitanes emerge. Currently the two Ortiz brothers, Javier and Reynaldo fulfill the role of capitanes (fig. 1.3).

Fig. 1.4 The Matachines de la Santa Cruz de la Ladrillera dance the son el Viejo, who is ritualistically "killed" and taken out of the circle by the capitanes. 2018. Photo by Norma Oralia Ortiz.

The dancing is physically demanding, with some sones lasting up to thirty or forty-five minutes, depending on the number of dancers participating. Due to the endurance required, the older dancers tend to not dance every *son*; instead, they selectively participate in the introductory dance and in La Despedida (the final dance). As they age and are no longer able to physically perform the long dance segments, they transition into other roles within the group; some take on roles as musicians or the role of el Viejo (fig. 1.4). The women become helpers in the kitchen or become involved in constructing the dance nagüillas, or skirts, and embroidering the vests.

The object of veneration, a wooden cross, hails from Las Minas as well. The story is well known, and most, even those who did not come from Dolores, acknowledge Las Minas as the root site of the tradition. Some of the elders I first spoke to, and who have since passed away, remembered the fiesta in Dolores and their pilgrimage or procession up the hill to where the Holy Cross permanently stood. Since there are two crosses, one in the Mother Cabrini Matachines group and one in the Ladrillera Matachines group, I venture to say that one cross probably came with the Martínez family when the first exodus happened in the thirties, and perhaps a second was brought by the Flores family that came later in the 1940s and who settled in the neighboring barrio of Cantarranas. After all, as Alfonso Peña (1972, 3) notes, there were two crosses in the area of the coal mines—one in Canel and one in Dolores, Texas. This would make sense because that second cross is much smaller than the one that the Ladrillera matachines venerate. And since both groups hold that theirs came from Las Minas, it is entirely plausible. Also, there are two *capillitas*, or small shrines: one that was until recently housed in a lot next to the Flores family's home on Boston Street in the Barrio Cantaranas and the other one on Camp Street in the Barrio de la Ladrillera behind the Ortiz family home; it is the group of matachines who dance at the latter that is the object of this discussion. The Flores family, as of this writing, has stopped celebrating the fiesta and the dancers have joined with the Ortiz family troupe.

Early Research with Elders

I was a graduate student in the mid-1970s when I stepped into the small home that consisted of three rooms of a faded blue frame-house, a shotgun style home with a neatly swept yard full of aromatic herbs—*romero*, *yerbabuena*, *manzanilla*, and others I didn't recognize. Doña Sarita Liendo (1892–1989) welcomed me to her humble home in the Ladrillera neighborhood on the banks of the Rio Grande River in the spring of 1975. She welcomed me as kin, for one of my sisters is married to one of her grandsons. At the time I was not very aware of the matachines, but I was talking to elders about La Pastorela, the traditional shepherds' play that was to be the focus of my dissertation. We chatted for what seemed a brief time, but suddenly I noticed that the sun had set and we had been *platicando* for hours. That afternoon, in one of my first talks with her, Doña Sarita whetted my appetite to know more about the matachines, the dance group I had first encountered as a child living in the barrio Cantarranas. But matachines dancing was not my focus on that day as I already mentioned; although we did talk about *mojigangas* (skit performances) and other traditional celebrations the community engaged in, we didn't dwell long on them as my focus was the Christmas shepherds' play for my dissertation research. When I left, Doña Sarita offered me plastic bags full of herbs—some fresh, others dried—that she said I should take with me back to Nebraska for the winter. I did and often, back in Lincoln, I would sip my chamomile tea and think of her and her simple home with the chicken coop in the yard and the rooster crowing, the neighborhood dogs barking, and the *capillita* (small shrine or chapel) de la Santa Cruz.

When I returned to Laredo in 1980 to teach at Laredo State University, I continued the research into the cultural practices of the community and attended the Matachines Fiesta de la Santa Cruz every May and in December when they danced for the Virgen de Guadalupe. In 1987, while doing field work for the Smithsonian American Folklife Festival, I returned to Doña Sarita for information. She confirmed the stories I had collected from others about the move from Las Minas and added some information. Subsequently, I spoke to various participants whose families had come from Las Minas. Doña Sarita exemplifies the process I am describing of how the tradition is transmitted and how the gender-stratified roles for participants sustain the community's engagement, incorporating an intergenerational network of collaboration and a faith-based commitment to dance and honor la Santa Cruz. She embodied the cultural memory of the move from Las Minas and was a pillar in the community; moreover, she had a key role in the fiesta as the person in charge of "dressing" the cross.

Through my intervention, the group was invited to attend the American Folklife Festival, as it was called then, for two weeks—the last week of June and the first week of July—in Washington, DC.

Although she was glad the group was traveling to DC for the festival, I could tell Doña Sarita had reservations; in May she looked into my eyes as we sat on a wooden bench in the *terreno* waiting for the dance to begin and said, *"Con o sin dinero, los matachines bailan"* (With or without money, the matachines dance). For years I pondered what that meant, for at no time had I intimated that they were being paid to dance, knowing that for them the tradition is sacred and is done with prayerful intention; it is never lucrative. Perhaps she thought that their participation in the festival in DC meant the group was deviating from that and were becoming a spectacle to be performed for pay. Years later, after she had passed away, I realized that she was reminding me, the researcher, that the community was there before I began my work and would be there after I had left; whether they were paid or not, whether I was there or not, they would continue with the dance. Throughout my pláticas with Doña Sarita, she often expressed not only a nostalgia for how things used to be but also a kind of acceptance of how time moves on and things change. She was glad women were dancing, for example, but sad that the cross was now dressed in artificial flowers and not the aromatic herbs and fresh flowers as in her youth.[7] Her wisdom and insight have sustained my work on the group and their history all these years, and I am forever grateful to her for her generous spirit.

When I first spoke to Doña Sarita, she was already an octogenarian, and so were others in the community, like Enrique Villarreal, who used to be the one to play the violin for the fiesta. Both of these elders are long gone, as are those of a generation later, like Doña Sarita's children, Isaac and Leonides Liendo. The Ortiz family is currently in charge of the fiesta; several generations of Ortizes have also danced and cared for the tradition, such as Florencio Ortiz (d. 1993) and Arquilino González (1935–2004); the former led the group until his passing in 1993, and the latter played a key role as the drummer and also was instrumental in preparing the nagüillas for many in the group.

The elders in the community are passing on, those who are my age and even younger. At seventy-six I have been attending and studying the fiesta for more than half my life. I have grown old with them. On a recent *plática* with Teresita González (2021), one of the main collaborators in my work, she expressed a similar nostalgia about how things have changed and expressed a similar faith in the persistence of the tradition.

Barrio de la Ladrillera / Santa Cruz

In my work with the Matachines de la Santa Cruz, I have found that the communal bond that exists in the community, the local barrio, forms a strong social bond and that the dancing is integral to the cohesion that exists. The elders sustain the social structure via their involvement in the church-sanctioned activities at nearby Holy Redeemer Church or Mother Cabrini Church. While my focus here is the barrio de la Santa Cruz, formerly known as La Ladrillera, I have observed a similar situation existed with the Cantarranas matachines. David Maldonado Jr. (1975, 213) noted that "the Mexican-American family has traditionally been characterized by its pattern of extended relationships." He further noted that the extended family structure was in a state of transition (214). Writing in the 1970s, he predicted the shifts that have indeed occurred in the larger Chicanx community, yet in the case of the matachines community in Laredo, the shift has not been swift and perhaps not even palpable, as I observed in 2019 when I attended the last in-person celebration.[8] The families sat in clusters around the elders and the roles they played were the same that their parents or in-laws had played. For instance, the dressing of the cross, as I will discuss below, has been passed from mother to daughter or to daughter-in-law for generations. These familial roles reinforce the bonds and solidify the persistence of the tradition within the community. One of the preeminent scholars who looked at aging in the Chicanx community, Martha Sotomayor (1971, 321), found early on that "the aged are greatly respected among Mexican Americans; positions of authority are assigned to them regardless of their sex." I observed the same situation in the matachines community, albeit with some changes due to the movement of some of the families away from Laredo. Nevertheless, in the groups that moved to Dallas or San Antonio, the tightly knit extended family persisted. Sotomayor further developed a view of the barrio, calling it "a supportive and flexible structure assuming functions in dealing with the environment and with the emotional and psychological aspects of the family unit and individuals" (312). In her pioneering work on the elderly, she laid the ground for others who looked at the impact of cultural change on the Chicana/o/x elderly. As Frank Cota-Robles Newton and Rene A. Ruiz (1981, 56) noted, "A barrio may be psychologically beneficial to elderly, relatively unacculturated Chicanos." They further concur that "a barrio is a place where the traditional culture is preserved: (1) It provides a sense of community, a sense of cohesion and belonging; (2) it is a secure place where recent immigrants can adapt gradually; and (3) in general, it can shield the individual from discrimination and the negative influences of modernization."

While the second item on their list may not apply to the matachines group, as they are not recent immigrants, I submit that the matachines community does indeed "provide a shield" as well as a strong "sense of community, a sense of cohesion and belonging" (56). The apparent resistance to modernity and the group's resistance to the forces of acculturation, in my view, are in large measure due to the dance tradition, a faith-belief system that upholds the individual within a community of caring along with strong extended family ties.

Dancing in community year after year establishes a bond that is at once tenuous and sustained. It is tenuous because the dancing is entirely voluntary and decided upon by the individual dancer. Moreover, it is a commitment to dance not just during the fiesta and in December for Our Lady of Guadalupe but even for special celebratory events. Many a dancer will vow to dance for a number of years, or even for life in thanksgiving for a favor granted, health restored, or for an accomplishment like a graduation or a mortgage paid off. In some cases, a member of the community who doesn't dance will instead host the matachines for dinner and a Danza de Matachines, and invite neighbors and family. Most often the dance takes place in the yard or in a space set aside for the event in the home. A make-shift altar is usually set up with the statue or image of the saint being honored in a prominent position. Be it Our Lady of Guadalupe or San Judas Tadeo, the dancers will perform the same sones, but in a much-shortened format. In sacralizing the space, the dance serves dual purpose as it allows the homeowner, invariably an elderly couple or single persons—widows or widowers, most often—to share their good fortune with others in the community or to celebrate an accomplishment. Yet it is also sustained because the individual commitment is inextricably bound to the community through a series of life-change markers. Moreover, the dancers are also members of various church groups and social groupings whereby their participation is reinforced. A Guadalupana sodality member will invariably also be involved in the December 12 matachín dance and procession in honor of Our Lady of Guadalupe. In my view, above all else it is faith in the miraculous powers of the Holy Cross that sustains the tradition. Time and again I have heard of miracle cures or events attributed to the Holy Cross. Many dancers have vowed to dance for life in thanksgiving for having beat a cancer diagnosis.

A community built around an event that has been happening for over a century annually and where the families have histori-cal memory of their parents' and grandparents' participation tends to ensure permanence and an adherence to tradition. Both family bonds and social bonds such as *compadrazgo*—the kinship estab-lished through sponsorship during liturgical sacraments such as baptism, first communion, weddings, and the like—add to the infra-structure that keeps the group going, as does the fact that it happens within the confines of a geographic area. The matachines dance troupe constitutes a community, but it also is integrated into the larger neighborhood or barrio community. Dance as prayer repre-sents a strong and powerful cultural and faith-based glue that unites the community and allows the elderly to have a role and a space within the community.

Fig. 1.5 The author with Francisca "Doña Panchita" Ortiz, Florencio Ortiz's widow. Doña Panchita and Teresita González have been in charge of the kitchen, where neighbors and friends gather to prepare meals for the dancers. Photo by Elsa C. Ruiz.

Women's Work

I began this chapter looking at Doña Sarita Liendo and her participation in the fiesta. In my work with this group for the last forty years or so, I have found the women to be incredibly engaged, and whether they dance, like Teresita González, or don't, like Doña Panchita Ortiz, they perform critical roles in the fiesta (fig. 1.5). When I met Doña Sarita, she had been dressing the cross for several decades; her role of caretaker of the cross, as she explained, demanded that she be in charge of dressing the cross. A few years before her passing, when she was no longer able to perform her duties, her daughter-in-law Claudina Liendo (1930–2016) assumed the role. "That's the way these things are done," Teresita informed me when I asked how it was that the tasks got assigned. After Claudina passed away, it was her sister-in-law,

Carolina (1945–2020), who took over. In 2019 Sarita's granddaughters, Elodia, Claudina, and Cristina, and her grandson Isaac Liendo, stepped up to the task. I am certain that one person will emerge as the caretaker of the Holy Cross as the COVID-19 pandemic restrictions are lifted. Because it takes months of preparation—selecting the color scheme, saving money for buying the materials, and planning the design—"Vestir la Santa Cruz" (to dress the Holy Cross) is a great honor, and those in charge of this essential task for the fiesta do it as a form of prayer. Undoubtedly, it will be one of Carolina's daughters who will step up. Perhaps Elodia, who has been dancing since she was around five years old and whose child is now dancing; or perhaps it will go to Isaac, her brother, who seems to be taking greater interest in continuing the tradition and has been helping the Ortiz brothers as they get older and are less inclined to dance. In any case, the transition will happen organically and naturally from one to the next.

I now turn to two elderly female members of the group who have remained steadfast and continue to be the core of the organizing, Francisca Ortiz, Florencio's widow, who is affectionately known as Doña Panchita, and Teresita González, whose husband, Arquilino (1935–2004), was also instrumental in performing many tasks after he was unable to dance due to health issues. Doña Panchita never danced, yet she has been instrumental in the fiesta in a number of roles. Primarily, she and Teresita have been the ones to secure the city permit for the procession. In 2020, even though everyone kept telling them that they would not be able to secure the permit due to the COVID-19 restrictions, they still persisted and made a trip to city hall to ask. She told me that she had prayed that they would relent, but of course they didn't. The health risk was too high.

In 2021 they didn't even try, for they knew things were still not open and that the procession would not be able to take place. However, they did prepare a meal for the few dancers that danced *en el mero día para bailarle a la Santa Cruz* (on the very day to dance for the Holy Cross). It was a small gathering of the capitanes, a handful of dancers abiding by the safety guidelines of no more than ten, gathered in the *terreno* to dance. In 2022 the Matachines de la Santa Cruz were back in full force, albeit with a smaller group of dancers and masked. A number of elderly women who have stopped dancing—or who never danced themselves but functioned as support for their family members who dance—and have taken on other tasks must be acknowledged for their work in keeping the tradition going.

Another key role that the women play is that of organizing the meals. In 2019 the fare was chicken salad sandwiches and punch—a drastically different offering from the elaborate brisket or mole or some other festive food that is more common during the fiesta. Doña Panchita's kitchen is a lively place during the fiesta as up to eight or ten women are engaged in food preparation of the traditional meal that is offered to the dancers. Different women come and go and young children are underfoot all the time as the adults are engaged in the cooking and serving of the plates. The dancers and their families sit at long picnic tables set out for the fiesta. Typically, it is the noonday meal on Saturday and Sunday and often a light dinner on Friday and Saturday. The donations pour in several weeks before the event. And the women under the direction of Doña Panchita prepare the traditional large *cazuelas* of food.

The elderly women often sit to the side while the younger women are the ones hustling to get the dancers fed. None of the dancers are engaged in the cooking, but several will remove their nagüillas and help distribute the plates heaping with food or tortillas or white bread, depending on what is being served, or pouring the punch or handing out sodas to the other dancers. While usually the dancers will be served first, I have also observed that the elders are served first and are seated in the choice spots. This simple observation reaffirms my argument that the practice exemplifies an Indigenous tradition, vestiges of which remain in simple behaviors or beliefs. Often entire families will sit together and enjoy the meal.

Fig. 1.6 Many matachín dancers embroider their names on their nagüilla. Celia "Chelley" Morales has been dancing since she was a child. 2023. Photo by Norma Oralia Ortiz.

But the dancers include the women too. Although prior to the 1960s it was an all-male troupe, nowadays the Matachines de la Santa Cruz include women dancers like Celia "Chelley" Morales, who has been dancing since she was a child; she's a direct descendent of Sarita Liendo (figs. 1.6, 1.7).

Fig. 1.7 Chelley dancing in her full regalia: red bandana and shirt and her handmade nagüilla, holding a *sonaja* (rattle) and the stylized bow and arrow noisemaker. 2023. Photo by Norma Oralia Ortiz.

I now turn to a bit of analysis of the fiesta in terms of its meaning for the dancers. As they go through the various stages, invariably some will drop out and not continue with the dancing, but many will remain loyal and dance from childhood until they are no longer able to do so due to ill health.

The Space of Nepantla

In Gloria Anzaldúa's concept of nepantla, as discussed in the introduction, the individual who is of mixed heritage, a mestiza or mestizo, could be in nepantla; similarly, something that is neither wholly one nor another but exists in an in-between space is also in nepantla. Nepantla is a space of growth and of transition according to Anzaldúa (2002, 1–2). In a certain way, for the matachines elders, not dancing and not participating in the myriad tasks can be said to be in nepantla, for they are no longer the ones dancing or performing the tasks that are essential for the fiesta; they are in a liminal space of transition but still form a core role for the fiesta. Carolina Liendo, who had been battling cancer, was in 2019 still attending the fiesta, helping her grandchildren prepare to dance and carefully assisting her daughter Elodia as she donned her nagüillas. While they may be wholly unaware of the concept, the once-dancer is now more than aware of their nonparticipation and that they are, as Teresita puts it, "mas pa' 'lla que pa' 'ca" (*más para allá que para acá*; more over there than over here), meaning that death is close at hand. Of course, the idea of death looms large as the community's health challenges are severe. The way the elderly approach death is similar to how they approach the dance: with prayer. If the nepantla stage is a transition and a place for transformation, the matachines elders are preparing and arming themselves for that through the fiesta.

At La Despedida, when the dancers and the devotees of the Holy Cross come together to close the fiesta, as it were, the prayers are powerful reminders that in the cycle of life and death, they are acknowledging the imminent future while praying for life for one more year to see and be at the fiesta one more year. In a sense, the fiesta functions as a life-marker, and at first I found it odd that so much revolved around the date of May 3. One couple felt blessed when their daughter, Cruzita, was born on that date. Just recently I found out that the mother of my sister's best friend growing up, Diana Vigil, had passed. Gloria Liendo Vigil died, her daughter suspects, of COVID on May 3, 2021—the day of the Holy Cross. Gloria was from the matachines community, and the significance of her death date cannot be overstated. May 3 is not on the official Catholic Church liturgical calendar, but it exists in the folk tradition and may have at one time been a feast day. When I first talked to Doña Sarita Liendo, and later to Florencio Ortiz, they both retold the story of how Santa Elena had found the true cross in the Holy Land and how Romans were converted thanks to the cross. The matachines had inherited the Holy Cross, and it was their duty to dance in her honor. Some dancers even call themselves soldiers of the cross.

Elsewhere I have written about the celebration of the Holy Cross and of its significance as a spring ritual in Spain (2012), where the tradition exists in Andalucía and in La Mancha. The practice of dressing the cross had waned, but recently there has been a resurgence, and neighborhoods compete to have the best-dressed cross. Even in small villages in La Mancha, I have seen a dressed cross in the plaza for a celebration that nowadays usually happens on the Sunday closest to May 3 and not on the day traditionally celebrated. Córdoba is notorious as one of the Andalusian cities where the feast is celebrated most extravagantly; the feasting goes on for three days. Other communities in Spain are also reviving the festival, yet in none of these do they have matachín dances.

Conclusions

In the twenty-first century, as more and more cultural practices in Chicanx communities are being commodified or transformed by the forces of capitalist interests—I am thinking here of the tremendous growth of the Day of the Dead celebrations of the last ten or twenty years—the Matachines Fiesta de la Santa Cruz remains solidly grounded in a small geographic space in Laredo, Texas. Not too long ago, the very popular Ballet Folklórico de Amalia Hernández added a matachines dance number to their repertoire of traditional dances from Mexico. Like the other numbers, it has been transformed with a choreography and costumes that are more for spectacle than for traditional accuracy. Just like they perform the Deer Dance from the Sonora/Arizona region, they are now performing matachines. In a way it is a testament to the way the tradition has gone mainstream; almost every community in Mexico has a group, and often more than one as each parish establishes a group. In San Antonio the missions—a designated historical heritage site under the supervision of the US Park Service—have added matachín dance groups, and at least one more traditional group that has been in the area for many years objects to how the dance appears to be more for tourist consumption than for prayer. In Kansas City I documented ten troupes, all of which remain firmly rooted in the community and, I suspect, would dance without church sanction.

The Laredo Matachines de la Santa Cruz de la Ladrillera may go that route, especially because Holy Redeemer Church is not much interested in the group. The relationship fluctuates according to the priest that is assigned to the church; if it is someone who knows the tradition, in other words—a Mexican or Mexican American priest— then more than likely that priest will be more amenable to the dance coming into the church, and he may even go to the *terreno* to offer a blessing or pray a rosary. But more often than not, the priest is not familiar with the tradition and will not be overly supportive of the troupe. The Holy Cross chapel—not the *capillita* where the group dances but a nearby chapel—is under the auspices of Holy Redeemer Church, and finally, with much sacrifice and lots of fundraising, the community was able to replace the building with a proper chapel to hold services. But it is a long way from being the church that many in the community want it to be. Nevertheless, on December 12, that is

Fig. 1.8 Reynaldo and Javier Ortiz inherited Florencio's devotion. The brothers have been dancing since they were boys and are the current capitanes. 2018. Photo by Norma Oralia Ortiz.

where the procession begins for the dancing in honor of Our Lady of Guadalupe as it winds its way to Holy Redeemer Church.

Florencio Ortiz was buried with his nagüilla in his coffin, as had been his wishes. Once a matachín, always a matachín; that is how the dancers see themselves. As I have outlined in this discussion, the matachines in Laredo, Texas, are a close-knit community that cares for the elderly members of the community. As members of such a faith-based community, fully devoted to the Holy Cross, they follow a self-selected transition along a pathway from dancer to helper and wise adviser, fulfilling different needs along the way. The matachín dancers and the members of the community who support the dancers go through the life-cycle transitions: beginning in childhood and on through to old age, as members of the Matachines de la Santa Cruz, they are embraced by the dance troupe and feel that they are home in their barrio and in their faith; thus, they have a sense of security and of belonging.

Fig. 1.9 During the May 3 fiesta, dancers kneel in front of the cross at the *terreno* on Camp Street. 2023. Photo by Norma Oralia Ortiz.

When the brothers Florencio and Pete Ortiz died, some thought the tradition would falter and perhaps not go on, but his sons have stepped up and have kept it going. As a folklorist working with a sentipensante theoretical lens, I cannot help but celebrate the way the community bond reinforced by the dance sustains and provides comfort in difficult times. Faith, belief, and commitment to the tradition keep it alive. During the COVID-19 pandemic, the group held together. And in the midst of the pandemic, in 2020, the group received national recognition from the NEA as recipients of the National Heritage Award, the highest honor a traditional artist can

Fig. 1.10 A group photo of the Matachines de la Santa Cruz on the seventy-fifth anniversary of the troupe's residency in Laredo, Texas, where they settled after migrating from Las Minas, upriver. They are wearing the traditional red top or vest and the nagüillas. 2014. Photo by Norma Oralia Ortiz.

receive. Because we were still under the shadow of COVID, they did not travel to Washington for a ceremony, as the NEA held a virtual celebration instead. The video shows the challenges of presenting the tradition when the fiesta was not officially held. Using some historical photos and video from the documentary produced by Marlene Richardson they were introduced to those in the webinar.[9]

Throughout the many years of my engaged scholarly work with the matachines, I have developed deep friendships with the members of the Ortiz family. We have attended each other's celebrations and funerals; our families remain intertwined in a number of ways. The special bond that has developed goes beyond that of researcher and collaborator. As I continue to work on the book project, I fear that I will never finish it, for the research never ends. And yet I know I must, for them and for myself. I promised that I would and I have, but I also need to publish and offer them a tangible product

for all the time that they have spent teaching me about the tradition.
A true feeling/thinking exploration into the meaning of the tradition
leads me invariably to a truth not often acknowledged, although
sometimes spoken: we researchers, folklorists, are shaped by the
work we do, touched by the people we work with, changed by the
experience of documenting and analyzing the cultural expressions
of a community.

Chapter 2

La Quinceañera

A Sentipensante Folkloristics Reading of a Coming-of-Age Tradition

Latinas coming of age in the 1960s, as I did, faced numerous conflicts of identity and of allegiance. The way that our community celebrated *quinceañeras*, a young woman's coming-of-age ritual, for example, was often suspect by most of us hippie-thinking Chicanes protesting the Vietnam War, joining the farmworker movement for social justice, and protesting the established order of things in general. Despite this cultural dissonance—as Michele Salcedo (1997, xii) points out in the introduction to her book *Quinceañera! The Essential Guide to Planning the Perfect Sweet Fifteen Celebration*, we still held on to the traditions; we still celebrated our quinceañera and helped each other come of age in an era of turbulence and chaos. Our parents didn't quite know what to do with our rebellion, having themselves been raised in the patriotic fervor of post–World War II US affluence, even though things were not quite as rosy or affluent for Chicanas and Chicanos in South Texas.

I recall one afternoon in the midnineties—*estabamos* mami and her sister, Tía Licha, short for Eloisa—when Tía Licha claimed that things were much better in the 1950s. She missed the "good old days"—this coming from a woman who had been a part of the migrant stream working long, arduous jobs in the fields and canneries *en el norte* (up north) and a victim of forced sterilization *cuando los doctores* (when the doctors) tied her tubes. They were *platicando y recordando* (chatting and remembering). I remember thinking that I would perhaps one day look back at the sixties and seventies with similar nostalgia and think that those were the good old days. Well, here I am in the next century, and indeed I am thinking that those were the good old days. I am fully aware of the many changes wrought through the struggle, La Lucha, and recognize the many ways we have moved forward, and yet there's so much more to be done. This became glaringly clear during the 2016 election. Thinking about women's rites of passage— the erosion of some traditions and the changes that have occurred in these rituals—drives me to contemplate the aspects of these traditions that remain. It is with this intention that I write this chapter in *Fiestas in Laredo*. Just like the Matachines de la Santa Cruz, quinceañeras have been celebrated in Laredo for about a hundred years, and similarly the fiesta has changed over the years.

The quince or quinceañera is a traditional celebration of a young girl's fifteenth birthday. In South Texas it refers to both the celebration and the young honoree, while in other contexts, primarily in the Caribbean, the fiesta is called a "quince." In this chapter I offer a brief overview of the celebration's history, describe the tradition, and offer some thoughts on how these coming-of-age rituals—especially the markers of a change in social status—could be read as markers of a Chicana resistance, an inhabiting of what Gloria Anzaldúa (1987) calls nepantla, a place of transition that ultimately leads to change and transformation. I also apply a sentipensante folkloristics, one that unites the feeling and the thinking as an approach. Using sentipensante folkloristics, I therefore consider the celebration grounding my analysis in my earlier analysis of the tradition as a third-space event. This concept, along with Chela Sandoval's (2000) idea of third-world feminism, establishes what I and other scholars call a Third Space

Fig. 2.1 At the author's quinceañera, children from the neighborhood gathered for a photo in front of the house on San Carlos Street. Circa January 3, 1962. Photo courtesy of Norma E. Cantú.

Chicana Feminist (TSCF) approach that, now pushed further with sentipensante folkloristics, yields a more nuanced analysis. Additionally, I use a *testimonio* methodology that seeks to explore the theory in the flesh concepts that Cherríe Moraga and Gloria Anzaldúa first introduced in their groundbreaking book, *This Bridge Called My Back: Writings by Radical Women of Color* (2002) and that the Latina Feminist Collective articulated in their collection, *Telling to*

Live: Latina Feminist Testimonios (2001). As in the previous chapter, using testimonio allows me to insert my own experience even as I am describing and analyzing the celebrations I have witnessed as a scholar and simultaneously participating as a member of the community where the celebrations occur. It is not entirely an emic approach, for beyond the fact that I am a part of the culture where the fiestas occur, I am also integrating my own testimonio and pushing toward a sentipensante folkloristics. The strictly emic approach asks that the research be one with the cultural milieu. Furthermore, the research design or parameters come from within that same cultural world. In this chapter I delve into the *fiesta de la quinceañera* not only as a participant observer but also as a member of the cultural group; having had a quinceañera and offering my *testimonio*, I also deconstruct the elements inherent in the celebration.

The conceptual framework used for analyzing and marking changes in age, I submit, must be intimately tied to chronological, social, psychological, and emotional ages. In other publications (Cantú 2002; 2014) I analyze the two pivotal *edades* (ages)—fifteen and fifty—for they constitute bookends to a woman's life. Grounding the content on this chronological and sequential structure demands that I also disrupt it, and in those essays I integrated the analysis of the *quinceañera* and *cincuentañera* celebrations. Drawing from that earlier work, I am here expanding on and recontextualizing the coming-of-age ritual of the quinceañera as it happens in South Texas, especially in my hometown, Laredo, in the twenty-first century.

Although South Texas was part of the nation state of Mexico almost two hundred years ago, it remains culturally bound to its roots in Mexican popular culture. This colonized space presents a ripe terrain for study of cultural change as well. Tejano history makes the Tejanos of South Texas unique; this region, along with Northern Mexico, constitutes a *frontera* culture, as Arreola and Curtis (1994, 7) have established, a cultural region where traditional Mexican ways continue to dominate social, religious, and in some cases even political life. At the different stages of its history, the area of South Texas has

Fig. 2.2 Silvia Yolanda Carbajal Esparza's quinceañera with her full court of fourteen *damas* and fourteen *chambelanes* in 1958. Note the cocktail-length dresses and gloves. Photo courtesy of Sylvia Vargas.

undergone radical change; the movement of people back and forth across two nation-states has given the area a sense of transitoriness, but those who remain—those who are descendants of the original Indigenous groups, the newcomers who settled there in the 1750s, and those who have been there a long time—sustain the cultural life of the region and ensure the permanence of the traditional expressions such as the quinceañera.

The celebration is indeed transnational, and often it happens on both sides of the border, as can be exemplified by the mother and daughter celebrations that my former student Sylvia Vargas pointed out. She generously secured these photos (figs. 2.2, 2.3, and 2.4) of her family's quinceañeras. Silvia Yolanda Carbajal Esparza's fiesta was held in Nuevo Laredo at the Cueva Leonística in 1957, while her sister María del Carmen Gaona Carbajal's was held in 1977, also in Nuevo Laredo.

For this chapter I consider the period from about the 1930s to the present; my conclusions and analyses are garnered from scholarly

Fig. 2.3 María del Carmen Gaona Carbajal with her *damas* in 1977 in Nuevo Laredo. The print fabric for the *damas'* dresses was unusual at the time. The honoree is wearing white, the usual color for the quinceañera dress at the time. Photo courtesy of Sylvia Vargas.

Fig. 2.4 María del Carmen Gaona Carbajal with the cake at her quinceañera in 1977. Photo courtesy of Sylvia Vargas.

work and my own intimate knowledge of the celebration through participant observation and through my life formation. After this analysis using Third Space Chicana Feminism (TSCF) alongside the already discussed sentipensante approach, I conclude with a very brief discussion of the current state of affairs that raises questions as to the future of these celebrations. Given that border violence wreaked by the drug-trafficking cartels has increased over the last twenty years, I ask, Will these celebrations continue? As Elaine Peña (2020) does, I conclude that they will, albeit with marked differences; as they have changed in the past to accommodate the changing social, political, and cultural expectations of the people who live there, so they will change in the future.

I lay out the chapter's premises in a hybrid genre, a narrative that goes into the intimate and heartfelt experiences and is interspersed with both ethnographic data and historical facts that weave a tapestry made up of the concepts highlighted by the celebrations and by the shifts of a woman's social standing. Focusing on one key and iconic ritual that signals shifts in status for women, the quinceañera, I also explore the silences that signal shifts in social status. I present an analysis of the significance of the particular cultural expressions found in the birthday celebration. While considering other markers of entrance into adulthood, shifts in social status, and the change in cultural traditions and gendered expectations diachronically in the border town of Laredo, Texas, I ask the following key questions: What do the changes in the celebrations indicate in terms of the shifts in the status of Chicanas in the body politic? Does the celebration of such life-cycle markers impact the status of the individual within the cultural terrain of the border community? Do changes in the celebrations indicate changes in the individual agency and/or subject positionality of the inhabitants of the border? Each of these questions raises important points relevant to an analysis of the cultural and expressive life of the inhabitants of the border and can therefore reflect similar changes across cultures.

Theoretical Approach

The theoretical frame based on the work of Gloria Anzaldúa, which posits that certain cultural expressions exist outside the mainstream and within a liminal space and time, offers an exciting vantage point for analysis, especially insofar as women's rituals are concerned. This third space presents possibilities but also challenges the integration of the cultural expressions within the larger panorama of the United States. In the next few paragraphs, I define key terms that I will be using in the chapter.

Nepantla

The term *nepantla* may need not just translation but also a more nuanced definition than I have heretofore been using. Anzaldúa uses the term to describe a late twentieth-century context of hybridization, but the word's etymology resides in Nahua thought from more than five hundred years before. Néstor García Canclini (1995) and Walter D. Mignolo (2012) also work with a similar concept of cultural overlap or synthesis. García Canclini's "cultural hybridization" refers to a particular cultural expression that "materializes in multi-determined scenarios where diverse systems intersect and interpenetrate" (53). Mignolo's project is more expansive; it began with the publication project *Nepantla: Views from the South* (Mignolo and Nouzeil 2003) and has evolved into a web dossier, "Worlds and Knowledges Otherwise" (n.d.). As he explains in the editorial note announcing the closure of the publication of *Nepantla* and the beginning of the website, the new project "could not be aspired to within the mono-topical or universal cosmology often referred to as 'Occidentalism' or 'modernity,'" and in the new *Worlds and Knowledges Otherwise*, "*Nepantla* and *nepantilism* are concepts implied in the very notions of *Worlds and Knowledges Otherwise*" (Mignolo and Nouzeil 2003, 421–22). Thus, I submit both that the term has widened in meaning from when it was first used in Náhuatl in the fifteenth century to when Anzaldúa used it in the twentieth century and that it is still in flux and may come to mean something akin to hybridity but definitely not just that. In a way, my use of TSCF is rooted in the notion or concept that nepantla allows. In this brief discussion on key terms, I want to clarify the way I am using TSCF theory in my analysis of life-cycle rituals in general and in the quinceañera in particular.

Anzaldúa sees nepantla as a stage that is recursive and, in some ways, as a perpetual state that infuses transformative meanings for the psyche, in contrast to the concept of hybridity that Homi K. Bhabha (2004) and other scholars have posited. Scholars of Aztec thought, such as Miguel León Portilla (1990), explain the concept as a philosophical position that accepts two seemingly opposing views that exist simultaneously. Historical documents trace the use of the term to Diego Durán (1994), who cites an unnamed Nahua man who claimed that worshiping both Christian and Aztec deities placed him in a state of nepantla; in other words, by following both his traditional Aztec belief system and the colonizer's Christianity, he is in nepantla. Anzaldúa then takes this concept and applies it to the Mestiza, the Chicana; thus I arrive at the discussion of a TSCF that I find useful in discussing liminal celebrations like the quinceañera or the wedding ceremony.

Third Space Chicana Feminism

Anzaldúa (2002, 1) claims that nepantla is a liminal space, an unknown space, "a *tierra desconocida* where transformation happens"; in my view the shift from one status to another is similarly achieved through a nepantla, a moving through a liminal existence. For Anzaldúa nepantla is where a rupture or a shift happens, I see the transitions offered by the life-cycle markers as places of awareness and of shifts in perception— both of how the woman is perceived and how she perceives herself in the world. A TSCF position then takes a woman through nepantla and into what Emma Pérez (1999) envisions in what she calls a "decolonial imaginary" that exists between the colonized and postcolonial states. These two key concepts—nepantla and TSCF—along with Chela Sandoval's (2000) concept of the differential consciousness allow for such shifts. Pérez (1999, 33) states, "Third Space feminism, then, becomes a practice that implements the colonial imaginary." Pérez's historical focus is the Mexican Revolution, where she finds that the decolonial imaginary exists for "the silent (to) gain their agency" (33). In her book *Methodology of the Oppressed*, Sandoval (2000, 2) provides a useful "apparatus . . . represented as first a theory and a method of oppositional consciousness . . . and . . . transforms into a methodology of emancipation." Because this "apparatus" constitutes the basis for what she had introduced as Third Space feminism in her essay "U.S. Third World Feminism: The Theory and Method of Oppositional Consciousness in the Postmodern World" (Sandoval 1991), I bring her into conversation with Anzaldúa and Pérez; thus, we have the TSCF theoretical lens through which to view the quinceañera.[1]

Quinceañera as Rite of Passage

I have been studying the coming-of-age ritual referred to as a quinceañera (fifteenth-birthday celebration) for about forty years; by "studying" I do not mean writing scholarly articles, although I have done that too, but I do mean observing, participating in, and thinking about the meaning such an event holds for the honoree and the community. Elsewhere, I have also discussed another life-cycle ritual, the *cincuentañera*—fiftieth birthday celebration—as a parallel phenomenon, since both signal a shift in a woman's life that brings a new set of responsibilities and a new status within the social structure of the family and the community (Cantú 2002, 30). The origins of both have been traced to the Amerindian custom of marking coming-of-age, usually at the onset of menses, and the passage into elderhood. Arguably, these celebrations could just as easily be attributed to Anglo-European customs that would signal a young woman's coming of age and thus her sexual availability; I am thinking here of cotillions, and even nineteenth-century customs of presenting young women in society.

While the celebrations I have studied are situated within a Mexican context, and more specifically a borderlands context of

Laredo in South Texas, they exist in what could be called pan-Latinx culture; that is, a similar expression, a quince, exists in other Latino communities, such as Caribbean (Cuban and Puerto Rican) and Central American communities, where a young woman's coming of age is also marked by a fiesta. The celebration is widespread in the US Latina/o community. In looking at these celebrations from a TSCF perspective, I now consider the essential components found in both and deepen the analysis of the rituals that exist in what are often both communal and individual celebrations in the US Latinx community.

For the quinceañera and the cincuentañera, the usual festival elements—music, food, ritual, and special dress—mark the sacred space of the fiesta that happens in the two traditional spaces for celebration: the church and the dance hall. Thus, they fulfill the need for spiritual or religious sanction; that is, the celebrations seek to fill a void wherein religious ritual and the social performative rituals (the dance), respectively, constitute aspects of the person's reality, her standing within the religious and the social realms of the community. According to the "Bendición al Cumplir Quince Años: Order for the Blessing on the Fifteenth Birthday" issued by the United States Conference of Catholic Bishops in 2007, the quinceañera Catholic mass offers the young woman the opportunity to reaffirm her baptismal vows and renew her faith. In the past most priests faced with a congregation whose young women wanted to celebrate their quinceañera in a traditional fashion developed an appropriate blessing that formed part of the quinceañera mass. A quinceañera is not one of the seven sacraments that the Catholic Church prescribes for its members—including baptism, eucharist, confirmation, reconciliation, anointing of the sick, marriage, and ordination—nor is it even a part of the liturgical calendar, or even strictly Catholic.[2] Yet the quinceañera mass is an essential element of the traditional celebration. In my observation, however, I have noted a decline in its importance; it has been less and less observed as young women eschew the church ceremony entirely. It is not unusual in Latine communities to have folk Catholic celebrations that are not necessarily church sanctioned.[3] The religious basis of the celebration reflects a syncretism as it embraces elements of both Indigenous and European origin, although these origins are also not widely recalled or known. The quinceañera occupies a liminal space within the registers of what constitutes a religious feast day. Perhaps this is due to the ways that the Catholic Church has both hampered and fostered the celebration.

Often the celebration, though, is allowed within the church ritual of the mass itself; it was not always so, as Norma Zuñiga Benavides writes of her quinceañera in the 1940s in her autobiographical book, *Holidays and Heartstrings: Recuerdos de La Casa de Miel* (Benavides and Azíos 1995). For her quinceañera, Benavides's family and friends gathered in the church to say a rosary and not a mass. Perhaps the mass was too akin to a wedding ceremony; the white dress and the diadem could be close to what a bride would wear. Benavides describes the event and notes that everyone joined, thus underscoring the idea that it is a communal and not merely individual event, although it is in honor of one single young woman who is now entering the ranks for adulthood.

The celebration typically begins when the young girl turns fourteen, as the family begins planning—and saving—for the big event. The invitations, usually sent out months in advance, are carefully selected and the wording worked over and decided upon. Most stores catering to the event include the invitation as part of the package. More recently, they are sending save-the-date cards ahead of the invitation, which now may include a gift registry. For mine we hand delivered the invitations printed by a family member in his printing business. We took the invitations personally to family and friends. My parents would not have even thought of mailing them. I recall that we made a special trip to Monterrey, 150 miles south in Mexico, to deliver invitations to my dad's family there.

To assist the family planning a quinceañera, a number of publications have sprung up, such as Michele Salcedo's (1997) *Quinceañera! The Essential Guide to Planning the Perfect Sweet Fifteen Celebration* and the Catholic-sponsored Mexican American

Cultural Center's publication (Erevia 1980). The former serves as a guide to the parents and the honoree as they plan the fiesta; the latter serves as a guide for a church-sanctioned mass liturgy. Some dioceses allow the priests to conduct their quinceañera celebrations as they best see fit, so some churches will have an annual celebration in May honoring all the parishioners who have turned fifteen the previous year; in a way these community-wide celebrations were supposed to help the financially strapped families of the quinceañeras. Apparently, this practice has all but stopped as the individual families sought to host their friends and family for the celebration. As an aide to the many parishes that were offering the quinceañera mass, Sister Angela Erevia (MCDP) prepared several handbooks (1980, 1985, 1992, 1996) to offer guidance to parishes and families as they prepare the religious ceremony within the Catholic Church. Obviously with the internet coming into the picture, multiple websites offer guidance, such as the most popular, Quinceañera.com, which offers a section called "Understanding a Catholic Quinceañera Mass." Holy Family Church in Pasadena, California, offers a package at a cost of almost $1000 for those who are new or nonparish members ("Quinceañera," 2019). This package covers the parish fees, including the altar servers. Not all families include the church ceremony. Some families celebrate two siblings whose birthdays are close with one fiesta. The Needham Guerrero family is one such family. Sisters Kassandra and Hailey Needham are a year apart and celebrated their quinceañera together (fig. 2.5).

On any given Friday and Saturday evening from Manassas, Virginia, to Atlanta, Georgia, from Omaha, Nebraska, to Fresno, California, young Latinas are celebrating their fifteenth birthday with a quinceañera mass surrounded by family and friends. The Church insists on focusing on the responsibility of the young woman, and some parishes require the young woman and her court, as the members of the party are called, to attend classes for a few weeks before the celebration. In her work on the tradition in Chicago, Chicana anthropologist Karen Mary Davalos (1996, 110–11) noted

Fig. 2.5 Kassandra and Hailey Needham, with their parents Justin Needham and Nancy Guerrero, at their joint quinceañera in 2023. Photo by Elva Margarita "Maggie" Martínez.

that the church uses the occasion for socializing the young woman in proper behavior and instilling a cultural identity. Other actions and artifacts signal the religious meaning of the celebration. For instance, one of the honoree's relatives is selected as the *madrina de medulla*, the sponsor for the religious medal. The medal is usually of the Virgen de Guadalupe, thus reinforcing the connection with the Indigenous, for Guadalupe, the Indigenous, dark-skinned Madonna, appeared to Nahuatl-speaking Juan Diego in sixteenth-century Mexico. I have also witnessed quinceañeras where the combination of Indigenous and Catholic ceremony elements blend. Should the family choose not to have a mass of thanksgiving, for whatever reason, it is often the case that a deacon or priest offers a blessing for the young woman, as was the case of one such celebration I attended in San Antonio,

Texas. In some cases the Church requirements make it difficult for the young woman to go through with the traditional quinceañera. Tradition bearer and National Heritage Award honoree Eva Castellanoz tells of her disappointment with the church in Nyssa, Oregon. In her book on Castellanoz, *Remedios: The Healing Life of Eva Castellanoz*, Joanne Mulcahy (2011, 44) writes about the young woman whose quinceañera encountered resistance: "Had she completed the required religious preparation, she would've been seventeen by the time she could celebrate her fifteenth birthday."

From a TSCF approach, we can deduce that the religious markers for the quinceañera are there to instill some restraint and to curtail the young woman's sexuality; in essence, the celebration signals her coming of age to mean that she is now of marriageable age.[4] Elsewhere I have explored how this liminal space for the quinceañera constitutes a passage between one clearly defined status (childhood) and the next (adulthood). But the religious and more sacred aspects of the celebrations give way to a more secular and social event; in fact in many instances, it is the dance and the music where things are played out and where the societal expectations are ritualized. In other words, many quinceañeras in the twenty-first century don't have a religious ceremony in the church. The social dancing that occurs both in choreographed and free form during the celebration signifies another third space in these celebrations, as often the deacon or some other church leader, sometimes even a priest, will offer a few words and an elder, usually a relative of the honoree, will deliver a toast. But it is the dancing that seems to have transformed into the ritual action that signals the shift to adulthood.

Dancing

Someone observed that often quinceañeras are where young people learn to dance. Indeed, the dancing is one of the quinceañera's celebratory elements where young people perform adulthood. *El baile* (the dance) includes dancing and music and happens in a special space,

a dance hall, *el salón*. The fiesta is the culmination of a series of steps
that began months before. The quinceañera and her mother select a
theme and colors for the decorations, and usually the color theme
is carried throughout from the church to the salón and is dictated by
the dress; the color also determines what the *damas*—the "court"
of fourteen young women who accompany the quinceañera—wear.
The choreography is an essential part of the dance. Salcedo (1997)
devotes an entire chapter to the choreography (105–17) and another
to the music (119–33). Such attention to these elements indicates that
they are metacomments on the event itself. The quinceañera dance,
often professionally choreographed, signals the honoree's new status
through a brief ritual where the *madrina de zapatos* presents her with
her new heels and she changes footwear, from flats to heels. Dancing
to a live band (or sometimes to a DJ), the young woman dances with
her father (fig. 2.9), then with her *chambelán* (fig. 2.8); finally, the
entire court—*damas* and *chambelanes*—performs the choreographed
dance. The quinceañera and her father invariably dance to a waltz.
Other common songs are Julio Iglesias's "*De niña a mujer*" (from
girlchild to woman) or similarly appropriate pop songs. Another
popular choice is a country music number, Tim McGraw's "My Little
Girl." At one quinceañera I attended, the father visibly shed tears as
he danced with his daughter to this poignant song. More commonly
these days, the father-daughter dance is followed by the members of
the entire court joining the honoree and her *chambelán* to do a choreographed dance to the honoree's favorite hip-hop song. While the usual
corte (court) is comprised of fourteen female teens and their male
escorts, variations exist where fewer *damas* and *chambelanes* participate or where it is an all-male corte. In Kamilah Rendón's case, the
court was just males (fig 2.6), but her girlfriends surprised her with a
choreographed dance (fig. 2.7).

So far we have been focusing on the elements surrounding the
individual, the honoree, as she performs her role at the center of
the celebration. I have been highlighting, however, that the family
and friends, especially the immediate family and the *madrinas*

Fig. 2.6 Kamilah Rendón with her all-male court at the church for her quinceañera in 2024. There's a similar photo of them at the salón. Photo by Miguel de la Garza, courtesy of the Rendón family.

Fig. 2.7 Kamilah Rendón's girlfriends were not *damas* in her court exactly, but they performed a choreographed dance at her quinceañera in 2024. Photo by Miguel de la Garza, courtesy of the Rendón Family.

and *padrinos*, or sponsors, are an integral part of the celebration. It is the sponsors who make the celebration a communal one; the quinceañera's family and close friends either volunteer or are invited to help pay for certain elements, such as the cake or music, or to gift the honoree with particular elements, such as the religious medal, the tiara, the shoes, or the last doll. In discussing the various items that are under sponsorship within the context of the celebrations, we can see the communal aspect that the marking of a change in status entails. For instance, the cake— usually an elaborately constructed one that reflects the theme—may include a cake-topper appropriate for the celebration. The quinceañera's cake .is often adorned with Barbie-size dolls representing the *damas* dressed in similar dresses as the young women.

The marking of the occasion by inscribing the date and the name on various objects (from napkins to party favors distributed to guests) signifies that the occasion is indeed a life marker. A madrina may also be in charge of gifting an engraved cake server set that has the honoree's name, the date of the celebration, and the number *15*. Similarly, champagne flutes used for the toast are engraved with the honoree's name and the date of the celebration along with the number *15*. Speaking of the toast, the age of the quinceañera and her *damas* and *chambelans* demands that sparkling cider be served for the toast and not the hard liquor or wine that is served for the adult guests; the *padrinos de brindis* toast as guests raise their flutes filled with champagne or sparkling cider.

Another item that is stamped with the name, date, and *15* is the guest registry book. It is currently customary for the sponsors of the book and of the remembrance photo album to have it hand decorated by a seamstress with an elaborate cover. The quinceañera usually invites a family member as a sponsor for the *libro y rosario*—the missalette or Bible and the rosary—that she carries into church. The kneeling pillow, *el cojín*, is customarily carried by a younger sibling or a cousin of the quinceañera who places it at the altar where the young woman will kneel.

As I mentioned earlier, at one point before the quinceañera dances the traditional waltz, the *madrina de zapatos*, the "shoes sponsor,"

Fig. 2.8 Carolina Alicia Melendez dances with her escort, Alejandro Avila, her *chambelán*, as her all-male court looks on, March 12, 2023. Photo courtesy of the Melendez family.

publicly has the young woman remove the flats she has been wearing and switch to high-heel shoes. Elsewhere (1999) I have discussed the significance of the shoes as signifiers of the young woman's new status, ostensibly her more precarious status, as she can no longer confidently and easily walk but must learn to walk wearing high heels. The quinceañera shoes clearly signal the passage from childhood to womanhood, *de niña a mujer*. We can also now discuss the previously mentioned last doll, as this too is a clear symbol of the change in status. The *madrina de última muñeca*, last doll sponsor, will present the doll either right after the dance or right before the cake is cut. The doll typically wears the same dress as the damas or an identical dress as the quinceañera's.

The quinceañera will use flowers profusely as part of the celebration. The quinceañera carries a nosegay or bouquet that at one
time, just like a bride's bouquet, was traditionally prepared of waxed
flowers, but now more commonly it is a plastic or silk flower arrange-
ment; this is also sponsored by the *madrina de bouquet*, again often
an unmarried female close friend of the family and may be interpreted
as a foreshadowing of the bridal bouquet. Of course, in this case the
young woman does not toss it to the young women in attendance to see
who will marry next as is done in the wedding celebration. The flower
bouquet or nosegay that the honoree holds often repeats the color and
kind of flowers that decorate the church and the salón. I don't remember my quinceañera having flowers of any kind other than the regular
flowers adorning the church altar. Undoubtedly, if I had known at
that young age what would be my favorite flower, we would've used
them. As already mentioned, the song selected for the father-daughter
dance constitutes an important part of the ceremony. I now turn to a
discussion of the music used in other parts of the event.

Music

To pay for the expensive live band or even for a good DJ, two or
three different groups of *padrinos de música* may be needed: one
or two will pay for the church music that is often secured separately;
the dance music, which includes a live band or a sound system, may
require several folks pooling their money together; and finally, another
padrino/madrina will sponsor the mariachi band that appears as if by
magic at the conclusion of the dance—around midnight—and sings
Las mañanitas, the traditional birthday song, with everyone joining
in the singing in honor of the quinceañera. The timing may vary, but
the point is that the mariachi band adds a traditional musical element
to the event. The video recording services may also be sponsored
and may be quite costly. Undoubtedly, as in a wedding, planning the
music requires intense and time-consuming care by the honoree and
her family. Since the events are along the border, it is not surprising

that a blend of Spanish-language and English tunes are selected. The social-dance music is also rather standard and will invariably, because we're in Laredo, include a Cotton-Eye-Joe and more than one Selena song. Cumbias and Tejano predominate and invariably draw the older crowd to the dance floor while hip-hop and some contemporary pop songs like "Despacito" draw the younger crowd to the dance floor. Laredo is a dancing city, and many times I have noted the particular shuffle that accompanies the cumbia dance moves that propel most dancers around the dance floor counterclockwise while some couples choose to dance in the middle. The intricate footwork that accompanies the distinctive polka of certain Tejano tunes are best performed by older dancers—the honoree's parents, uncles, aunts, and even grandparents' generation.

The Dress and Other Apparel

The dress remains of utmost importance to the quinceañera—that is, the honoree—as well as to her family, as Rachel Valentina González has brilliantly demonstrated with her book chapter "Buying the Dream: Relating 'Traditional' Dress to Consumer Practices in US Quinceañeras" (González-Martin 2020) and in her book, *Quinceañera Style: Social Belonging and Latinx Consumer Identities* (2019). In my research I have explored the differences between the dress worn by the *quinceañera* in Mexico or in the United States as well as in Central America and in other communities. González has also done work in the area and has found that there are distinct differences among various groups of Latinas and the dress choices. While at one time the dress was a pastel color—or for Chicanas, white—it is now permissible to have print and loud bright colors for the dress. Furthermore, it is often the case that the dress is constructed in such a way as to be adapted for the choreographed dance. On several occasions I have seen young women wear demure long formal gowns to the church and then, at the time of the choreographed dance, remove the long skirt to reveal a short one. As a headpiece, the quinceañera will wear a *diadema*, or tiara, that matches the nosegay or bouquet. Eva Castellanoz, a master artist, creates these using the traditional dipped-wax flowers and prepares the young woman for the quinceañera in her community in Nyssa, Oregon. Joanne Mulcahy's book *Remedios: The Healing Life of Eva Castellanoz* (2011) tells of Castellanoz's deep commitment to traditional practices. She too has seen a decline in the use of the traditional *diadema*; the headpiece in times past would also have included a *mantilla*, or traditional lace scarf, but nowadays the *diadema* is all that is worn on the head.

Other Accoutrements

For quinceañeras the event also signals a time to use grown-up formal clothing and jewelry, including a ring, a pendant, earrings, and an ID bracelet (often called an *esclava*), that are traditionally gifted by various *madrinas* and *padrinos*, including the sponsors of the *libro de recuerdos* or the gold Virgen de Guadalupe medal.

The traditional quinceañera celebration has enjoyed a renewed popularity in recent years, as social media and marketing for the celebration attest. Perhaps it is the migrant community from Mexico and Central America that has revived the tradition in the United States, but it remains very popular with the nonimmigrant Latino community, especially with Chicanx communities in the Southwest that have celebrated *quinceañeras* since at least the late nineteenth and early twentieth centuries.

Insofar as the quinceañera celebrations often signal changes and commemorate shifts in status in Latina communities, one can easily gauge from these celebrations the sentiment of Latinas in terms of their social standing and the accoutrements that go along with the shifts. While not necessarily a major paradigm shift in terms of the ways that they will now be perceived, the celebrations do mark a change in status. Looking at the traditional and well-established quinceañeras, one can claim that they serve a function in the Latinx community: first, they honor women transitioning from one status to another at a critical age;

second, they bring the community together in celebration; and third, they attest to the social and religious palimpsest for the entire social contract among an ever-diverse Latinx community. From a feminist perspective, they may appear to be anything but feminist as they often reinforce strict gender stratification and restrictions, perhaps even being sexist in their portrayal of women as sexual objects. But I submit that the very act of proclaiming that they celebrate their age is an act of resistance and affirmation. Further, the celebrations exist and will continue to exist as parts of a technology of life that affirms identity and reinforces the communal bonds. The teenagers claim their space and their actions in asserting who they are and what they want. Recent actions by quinceañeras have highlighted political and social justice work. For instance, a group of young women donned their quinceañera dresses to protest Texas Senate Bill 4 (SB 4), a law aimed at banning sanctuary cities in Texas, in Austin in front of the state capitol.[5] Also, some quinceañeras have used their celebratory gatherings to register voters during an election season. The passage through nepantla only renders them stronger and gives them a clearer location from where to embark on the next stage of life. After her quinceañera the young woman becomes an adult member of the community, integrated into the life of the social group, and is expected to measure up to the responsibilities that her new status entails.

The quinceañera celebrations signal a change in status, true, but more importantly they provide a vehicle for recognizing and celebrating the various bonds existing in one's community, one's family, and one's social world, and more recently one's political world. The Chicana feminist third space that the quinceañera occupies easily shifts to a sentipensante and an entirely holistic view of the young woman.[6]

Now, where does this celebration come from? In my research I have found that the tradition—and by the way, the definition of *tradition* that I like to use states that it is a behavior or custom passed from one generation to the next informally and through word of mouth—is rooted in European and Indigenous practices.

From European court presentations—Spain, France, and Italy are the most relevant for our Mexican ancestry—we get the language and the practice of cotillions or debutant balls. From Indigenous coming-of-age rituals, we get the ceremonies and rituals grounded in coming-of-age rites. For instance, the Mescalero Apache—and I should remind you that the Coahuiltecan groups that roamed what is now Laredo were closely aligned to the Apache in traditions if not always aligned politically—four-day ceremony with ritual actions includes sponsors and community-wide feasting with special foods. Initiation rites welcome the young woman as an adult member of the group, and she is given responsibilities and is no longer considered a child. However, one key element is the timing: the Indigenous rituals occur at the onset of menses, right at the first menstrual period. In contrast, the quinceañera occurs at age fifteen. Why at fifteen? The best I have been able to find is that it is a reaction to the Mexican government declaring that a young woman at age fifteen becomes marriageable. My paternal grandmother, for example, married at age fifteen. Although this is no longer the age when young women are expected to marry, as it was in my grandmother's time, the idea that fifteen is a marker of increased awareness and a time for added responsibilities persists—driving a car, dating, attending dance events and parties, for example. In any case, the quinceañera signals a shift in status.

Quinceañera themes vary widely, from the most common—Cinderella—to masquerade, to winter wonderland, to Paris, Tejano, and Charro. For a while the Chola theme was popular—that is, the 1940s style of dress and music—but now there seems to be a preponderance of western and country-music-themed celebrations. The party package that families purchase usually includes everything, even the table decorations, but the church package is a separate expense.

After such a discussion of the tradition and its elements, I turn to a discussion of the transformation into a quinceañera celebration more suitable for our time and age, configured and reimagined yet adhering to the usual elements that constitute the celebration.

Transforming Tradition

When Norma Benavides observed her quinceañera with a rosary and a celebration in the 1950s, as she described in her family autobiography, *Recuerdos de La Casa de Miel* (Benavides and Azíos 1995), certain conventions governed the celebration. Many of these were still in effect in the 1960s when I celebrated my quinceañera, despite the variance due to class differences. But in the late twentieth and early twenty-first century, I observed a decided turn away from the elements that had dominated the celebration even as there seemed to be a return to the earlier ostentatious display of the family's financial means. The first palpable difference was the move away from the white dress to all kinds of colors and even prints. As noted above, González-Martin has studied the dress and its significance. A second major change was in the less frequent use of the religious or church ceremony. Many chose to just skip it and have the event at a secular, albeit social, space like a reception hall. Such seemed to be the practice at a Peruvian quinceañera held in Tulsa, Oklahoma, in 2015. A blogger chronicled the event and noted that the event included a priest's blessing and parents' speeches, but didn't mention a religious liturgical celebration such as a mass (Kingsley 2015).

Why is this shift happening? I am not sure, but I suspect it has to do with various factors surrounding the general decline in practicing Catholics even within the population that has had such a long tradition of Catholicism like the Chicane community. Another major shift is the transformation of the celebration into a political event. As I wrote in a previous publication, "Cultural displays such as the quinceañera serve as affirmations of ethnic identity and of resistance to outside cultural forces," and "as its ramifications play out along the US-Mexico border, the neo-colonial hegemony is both challenged and appropriated in these events . . . the fiesta de quinceañera offers a cultural practice as a site of resistance to these hegemonic forces" (1999, 80). I find the use of tradition to make a political statement hopeful. I am particularly glad to see the shift in traditions, especially those that

Fig. 2.9 Carolina Alicia Melendez dancing with her dad, José Melendez, March 12, 2023. Photo courtesy of the Melendez family.

might have had questionable value as promoters of social justice; the quinceañera, for example, could be viewed as antifeminist, as young women often perform traditional feminine aspects of womanhood (such as donning high heels) that would be anathema to feminist practices. Yet, as mentioned above, quinceañeras have lately taken advantage and made the celebration an occasion for voter registration or for political protest. While not commonplace, the use of the tradition can be for political performance, such as the aforementioned young Tejanas who, in response to the anti-immigrant senate bill in Texas in 2017, showed up in their colorful, billowing dresses wearing banners that read, "Democracy," "No SB4," and "Family Unity," among other slogans (Diaz 2017; Herman 2017).

In the midst of all this, I feel I must mention two celebrations that went viral: the quinceañeras for Maya Henry and for Rubi Ibarra García. The two couldn't be more different, and while I wish I'd been able to conduct fieldwork and actually attend these two iconic celebrations, I did not. I am therefore relying on the media and what has been documented using social media, principally Facebook, Twitter, and Instagram, for a description.

These two quinceañeras epitomize the ways the celebration exists in the twenty-first century with all the social media impacts. In Rubi's case, the celebration held in December 2016 was not meant to be such a spectacle. Rubi's father inadvertently posted a video invitation and it went viral. Over twenty thousand people showed up to their ranch near the small town of La Joya, San Luis Potosi, in Central Mexico. The extreme reaction resulted in unexpected consequences, including an accidental death. One person was killed at a horse race that offered a ten-thousand-peso prize. The music featured two bands, Los Cachorros and La Heredera. The food was traditional mole and chilaquiles (Primera and Toral 2016). In the case of Maya Henry, the multimillion-dollar celebration was held in San Antonio, Texas, and featured entertainment by Nick Jonas and Pit Bull, among others, including a full mariachi band, while the guests feasted on gourmet food (Bryant 2016). But these are exceptional celebrations; in Laredo, while the celebration may also be lavish and cost thousands of dollars, it remains rooted in the more traditional event as described above.

Conclusions

As I come to the end of this chapter, I want to reflect on what it means to "come of age"; in anthropological studies the idea is studied alongside biological coming of age (menses, for women). Van Gennep (1960, 68) makes a distinction between physical and social puberty that I find useful for discussing the quinceañera, which I have come to realize is more than just reaching an age; it is a matter of reaching a shift in status as well. In soma studies we look at the body and its narrative. I am focusing here on the onset of menses as a traditional marker of womanhood, but perhaps we can go deeper and look at various instances of how one comes of age. Mentally, studies have shown that

it is not until an average age of twenty-five that the brain is fully developed and we become mature; although, there is some polemic around
the difference between brain age and maturity ("At What Age is the
Brain Fully Developed?" n.d.). Emotionally, we could argue, some
never do achieve maturity, as they may not have had experiences that
would assist in the process. However, the young women who choose
to have a quinceañera celebration (or whose families insist on it) are
transformed. Perhaps because it is on the border, the normalizing of
the tradition constitutes a phenomenon not observed everywhere.
And even in Laredo, many choose not to celebrate and instead opt for
a car or a trip to Europe.

While in terms of the physical, the soma, we do establish that there
are biological markers for coming of age—body changes, for instance—
and we can argue that it is not always the case with other markers.
Would the sweet sixteen be a better marker? Or high school graduation
with its prom? Or in the case of Laredo, is the George Washington's
Birthday Celebration (GWBC) also a marker—especially for the
young debutantes? Is there an age when a person can be considered
an adult? Legal status is established at age twenty-one, for instance,
when one can legally purchase alcohol. Or eighteen for induction into
the military? I am not sure it is always that clear. So while the fifteen-
year-old young woman may be feeling mature, and while society
may now view her as a member of a different group—a group that
includes young adulthood—it may be that she is not quite ready to
make that leap. Yet the expectation is there. On the other hand, girls are
being pushed to act older and to perform their femininity at a younger
age. Thus, twelve-year-old girls will be wearing makeup and heels,
behaviors that would've been delayed until after a girl's quinceañera.
In a perhaps disturbing practice, I have now observed that young girls
turning five are celebrated with a similar fancy party. But such a discussion remains for a different project.

I suspect that quinceañeras who actually go through the rituals
associated with coming of age as played out in the ceremony and fiesta
feel more mature; I know I did. And along with that realization comes

the awareness of one's place in the social fabric of the community and one's obligations or duties as such. From a sentipensante perspective, the thinking-feeling subject is now aware of the emotional as well as the rational aspects that may at times diverge but more often than not are in sync. We may think and feel that we are now in an adult role, but certain societal restraints remain outside of the cultural expectations for Chicanas.

I conclude this chapter with an observation of how, from an Anzaldúan perspective, the threshold that a Latina crosses during her quinceañera symbolically may send her into the Coatlicue state[7]; that is, she may be feeling that she is not quite adult enough, but she is no longer a child and may then be in a quandary as to who she is. The chaos and turmoil that often accompany adolescence may compound the emotional precarity, and it is only through awareness and acceptance of every aspect of the self that some sense of transcendence is achieved. Often this difficult time is made even more so for Latinas who may be situated in school or social settings that exacerbate feelings of inadequacy or of not belonging. I know for me it was a time that required immense concentration and almost a molting, as I felt I left my old self behind and entered adulthood. Among the many factors contributing to such feelings were my status as the eldest of eleven children, the feelings of frustration as I always felt I wasn't quite good enough to be in the accelerated (now they call them gifted) classes, and the dubious honor of being smart. I knew I was smart, and yet my grades didn't always reflect that; I loved to read, and I found solace in books, but it was not an activity that was encouraged or that was valued by those around me—except at home, where my father read voraciously and our "homework" time was sacred. A feeling that something had changed pervaded the entire day of my quinceañera; wearing a glamorous white, poufy quinceañera dress and dancing my first dance with a boy—even though he was a family friend and we only danced the one dance out of courtesy, in obedience to our parents' wishes—it all meant I was now a different person. I remember changing out of that dress and donning a regular blue cotton dress for photos with the neighborhood kids (fig. 2.1).

The differences between the individual and family-centered quinceañera celebration and the matachines, a religious barrio-wide celebration, are clear, and yet in a sense they are both at the core of bringing community together and exemplifying the way Latinx groups perform and embrace their identity. The *abrazo*, the embrace, is wide and all encompassing.

Reynaldo and Javier Ortiz in the *terreno* lead the Matachines de la Santa Cruz in a *son* (dance). Photo by Norma Oralia Ortiz.

Javier Ortiz (in the foreground) and his brother Reynaldo lead the troupe in their dance of devotion outside of Holy Redeemer Catholic Church. The brothers have been dancing since they were boys and are the current capitanes. 2023. Photo by Norma Oralia Ortiz.

Matachines dance to and from Holy Redeemer Church in procession. 2023. Photo by Norma Oralia Ortiz.

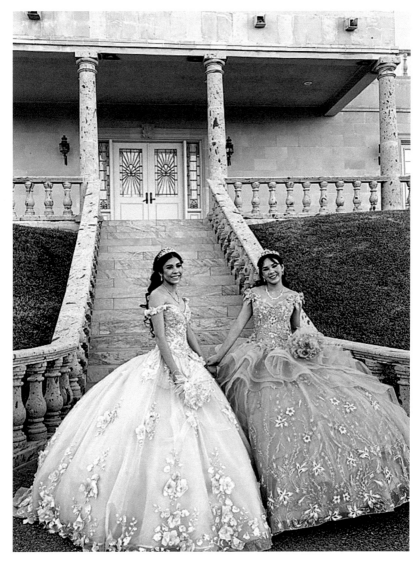

Hailey (in pink) and Kassandra (in blue) Needham celebrated their quinceañeras with a joint fiesta. April 2023. Photo by Elva Margarita "Maggie" Martínez.

Andrea Mía Contreras at the altar for her sixteenth birthday with her parents, Ángelica Marina Contreras and Ruperto Contreras III, at San Luis Rey Church. She celebrated her sweet sixteenth with all the quinceañera elements.

Ariana Botello at the Society of Martha Washington Debutante Ball in February 2023. Courtesy of Ariana Botello.

A still from the documentary film *Las Martas* (2014) shows Rosario Reyes, a debutante from Nuevo Laredo, onstage. Photo courtesy of Cristina Ibarra.

Another still from the documentary *Las Marias* (2014), this time showing a "legacy" debutante, Laurita Garza Hovel. Photo courtesy of Cristina Ibarra.

Chapter 3

Reenacting What Never Was

George Washington's Birthday Celebration

In my first memory of watching the Washington's Birthday International Parade, I am sitting on my father's shoulders, marveling at the prancing horses, the troupes of dancing children in colorful dresses, the soldiers and military tanks (that part was scary for a little girl). It was the 1950s, and I was around five. Most of all I remember the people, more than I'd ever seen in one place, swarming the streets of Laredo, Texas, my hometown. In elementary school we prepared for Presidents' Day (commemorating Presidents Lincoln and Washington) by coloring their portraits and hearing stories of these two men whom we honored on February 12 and 22, respectively. But Washington was always the one at the center of the main celebration when we attended the parade, went to the carnival, and enjoyed the city's fireworks. The fiesta happened on the Saturday closest to February 22. People from both sides of the Rio Grande/Rio Bravo celebrated Washington's legacy with military displays at events like the International Parade, the Air Force flight formations, the open house at Laredo Air Force Base (closed in the 1970s during Richard Nixon's administration) and

Fig. 3.1 This poster advertising the George Washington's Birthday Celebration in Spanish features Carlotta Rogers Warwick portraying Princess Pocahontas in 1916. Courtesy of the Webb County Heritage Society.

at city-wide events like Noche Mexicana, *la pólvora* (the fireworks), the carnival. As a teenager my favorite was the carnival, for it was where we would flirt with the guys from Mexico and enjoy the rides and the food. I would gorge on cotton candy and candied apples and feel the excitement of riding *el Mazo* or *la Rueda de la fortuna*, what

I learned to call the Ferris wheel. We played games at booths, hoping to win the giant teddy bear or some kind of knickknack or even a tiny pink or blue real live chick. Despite some vague feelings of unease, I happily enjoyed my community's annual festival without questioning or critically analyzing why we did what we did—indeed, not even acknowledging that it might seem an odd celebration for a city on the border that had a history that predated the founding of the nation.

In this chapter I offer an overview of the history of the George Washington's Birthday Celebration (GWBC), then I turn to some aspects of the fiesta that may offer an answer to the question I am asked anytime I talk about my hometown's celebration to outsiders: Why? I offer a cursory history of the celebration because as Elaine Peña (2020, 5) admits, it can be a daunting task, and I am not prepared to offer a more complete history at this time. Others have already done what I consider a more than adequate job of laying out the fundamental tenets of the celebration and its history. I will briefly mention the major contributors to establishing a history of the fiesta and then offer a context for the event as I see it from a folklorist's perspective, threading in some observations of the ideas I've been weaving in the previous chapters. In my discussion of the elements, the economic impact, and the ways place and space are configured during the celebration, I also provide a context drawing from my own memories of attending the annual event along with the concomitant characteristics that can be gleaned when looking at the fiesta itself.

History and Context

Prominent among historians of the celebration is local historian Professor Stanley Green, who was my history professor at Texas College of Arts & Industries (Texas A&I) at Laredo (now Texas A&M International University [TAMIU]) in the early 1970s. Green's (1991a, 1991b, 1992, 1993) Border Studies series documents the history of the celebrations via interviews and archival research. Professor Jerry D. Thompson (1986, 1991, 2011, 2015, 2017), another historian of South Texas, while focusing on the military history of the region, also includes references to the celebration. Elliott Young's (1994, 1998) articles also rely on interviews and intensive archival research to frame his historical perspective on the celebration.

Contemporary work on the celebration includes the superb work of Professor Elaine Peña, whose book *Viva George!: Celebrating Washington's Birthday in the Border* (2020) not only provides historical data but also analyzes key elements of the celebration using an anthropological and political lens. Peña's attention to the international or transnational aspects of the celebration and the contemporary pressure to shift long-held practices due to threats of violence and political turmoil speaks to the current status of the celebration. In many ways, *Viva George!* answers fundamental questions about the fiesta that had heretofore remained unasked as scholars merely traced the event across time and/or described the parts of the celebration. Young (1994, 1998), however, does delve into an analysis of the celebration's role in the community and why the nineteenth-century powers that reigned over Laredo imbricated the fiesta onto the city's life. Professor Stanley Green recently recorded a series of short TikTok videos posted by Webb County Heritage (2022a, 2022b, 2022c) on various aspects of the celebration. He spoke of how the celebration changed around 1901, pointing to the fact that Porfirio Díaz sent a Mexican delegation, thus turning the fiesta into a transnational celebration with visitors coming to Laredo from the south and the north. Mexican participants and the added political aspects of having trains full of visitors from both directions further influenced the festival (Webb County Heritage 2022b). In another episode, Green talks about how Laredo is an example of diversity and tells of how Laredo organized against the KKK; he reiterates what others have claimed about Laredo—that it is not racist and is indeed diverse (Webb County Heritage 2022c); Young (1998), on the other hand, provides evidence of the racism against African American and Indigenous peoples found in the late nineteenth and early twentieth centuries.

It was while researching the Matachines de la Santa Cruz in the early '80s, upon my return to Laredo, that I came upon the scant history of the GWBC in Laredo. I have found that often one line of research will lead to another; the rhizomic nature of research, if you will, leads a researcher from one line of inquiry or topic of research to the next. So it was for me. What I found included the still-dominant narrative that tells of how in the late nineteenth century, the San Antonio chapter of the Improved Order of Red Men helped Laredoans establish a chapter themselves, Yaqui Tribe #59. Why would they do that? Why would the elites want to identify as Indigenous? And who were these "red men" who felt impelled to impose such a celebration where before there had been harvest celebrations like the onion festival, or patriotic celebrations like the annual *El Grito* on September 15 celebrating Mexican independence from Spain, or the religious holidays with neighborhood processions like the ones for the feast of Corpus Christi at Christ the King Church? At the time, every parish held a fiesta for their saint's day—the *jamaica*, or what was known as *kermes*[1] in Mexico. The same *jamaicas* were held in conjunction with the fiesta since the outset. I remember the *jamaicas* at San Luis Rey Church, the parish where our family worshipped; it invariably meant music, raffles, and a number of vendors and stands where one could try one's luck and perhaps win a potted pothos plant—a Julieta that often was paired with another green leafed plant called a Romeo. These names spurred my imagination, and my mother's green thumb and baking genius provided many a plant for that booth or a baked cake for the cakewalk. But back to the most often asked question each time I present on the celebration: Why?

In retrospect, the group's motives are obvious. Laredo was simply too Mexican, too Indigenous, and they needed to jumpstart, to speed up our Americanization process, to more effectively erase the Indigenous and Mexican, to instill the settler colonialism[2] that made us "strangers in our own land," for after all, while we may be using dollars to conduct business, we were still calling them pesos. Our material reality reminded everyone we had been part of Mexico; only fifty years earlier, the Treaty of Guadalupe Hidalgo had made the Rio Grande the boundary between our two countries, severing the

FIB·22·34·LAREDO·TEX

Fig. 3.2 The members of the Improved Order of Redmen and Princess Pocahontas in 1934. Ermine Gass portrayed Pocahontas in 1934. Courtesy of the Webb County Heritage Society.

unified social entity that we were. From the outset it was a binational celebration, as the two communities were, as they are now, bound by strong family and cultural ties, although Green claims that it was not so until Porfirio Díaz sent a marching band to participate in the parade (Webb County Heritage 2022b). Here is how Elaine Peña (2020, 19) describes the 1898 celebration: "In February 1898, thousands of people from both sides of the US-Mexico border gathered in Laredo, Texas, to celebrate George Washington's birthday. Organized and promoted by members of IORM (Improved Order of Red Men) Yaqui Tribe no. 59, the two-day event featured a reenactment of the Boston Tea Party followed by a grand pyrotechnic show, an international parade, and a meet and greet in the middle of the bridge." She created this composite from intensive archival research and thus shows that the essential elements of the annual fiesta as we know it today existed from the outset. Peña, culling from laborious archival research, goes on to describe the 1898 mock battle and the tea party reenactment where members of the IORM Yaqui Tribe 59 fraternity members played all the roles; she also claims that "an earlier generation of border residents had commemorated Washington's birthday in 1870 with 'five races (foot and horse) and cash prizes'" (2020, 4).

Stanley C. Green notes that the earlier celebrations were mostly the soldiers at Fort McIntosh and local groups participating in a parade (Webb County Heritage 2022b); I would add that the celebration provided the local elites a venue for an ostentatious display of their status in the community and for reinforcing an Americanizing message that set in motion the staging of a reenactment of an event that never happened. I concur with Young that the political, economic, and military powers had much to gain by having the event happen despite its anachronistic logic.

Even as late as the early 1900s, some of the city business was still conducted in Spanish; perhaps it was the persistence of the Spanish language and Mexican cultural practices that impelled the powers that be—mostly immigrants from the north who spoke English and ruled alongside the local Mexican/Tejano landowners—that what was needed was a celebration, a fiesta to celebrate our American identity.

Members of the IORM Yaqui Tribe 59 seemed intent on celebrating even more dramatically with a zealous intent to ground the celebration in one important message: Laredo was part of the United States. Quoted in an article by Daniel Blue Tyx (2019), who wrote of the 2019 fiesta for the *Texas Observer*, a founding member, German immigrant Joseph Netzer, claimed, "It was our idea . . . that we should inculcate in the minds of the Laredo people the importance of observing American holidays and arouse a patriotic feeling to America and American institutions." As a folklorist who studies such events, I now appreciate that my hometown is only doing what other communities do and that it created a tradition that honors an imagined heritage for reasons that seemed plausible in the late nineteenth century and may seem dubious in the twenty-first century. The historical narrative remains steadfast and is drawn from the work of Wilcox, Green, and Thompson, and from the Washington's Birthday Celebration Association (WBCA) website ("History," n.d.).

While for this chapter I am particularly concerned with the GWBC fiesta in Laredo, it is worth noting that Laredo is not alone in celebrating with parades and presentation balls. Down the river, Brownsville celebrates Charro Days; about 150 miles to the east, Corpus Christi celebrates Buccaneer Days; and to our north, perhaps the most perplexing of all, San Antonio celebrates Fiesta to commemorate the battle of San Jacinto, the decisive battle of the Texas Revolution. I say perplexing because, while the others are celebrating an imagined event, San Antonio's Fiesta commemorates a real historical event, the Battle of San Jacinto, the decisive battle that led to Texas's secession from Mexico and eventual annexation by the United States. But that is another story, and other scholars have grappled with making sense of the fiesta where a mostly Mexican town celebrates the defeat of Mexico. As Peña (2020, 129) points out, "The Washington's Birthday Celebration may be idiosyncratic and highly particular to the two Laredos, but border enactments are not." She posits the idea that "recognizing a border enactments' scaffolding potential can innovate how we think about and tackle global challenges linked to border security, immigration, and trade" (129–30). It is conceivable that Peña's observations about the GWBC are also applicable to these other border enactments. In fact, there are social and political ties among these and others as many of the debutantes and the "royalty" associated with these fiestas travel to participate in each other's events. The parade in Laredo features floats sponsored by these other events, for instance, and San Antonio's Rey Feo participates in various GWBC events like the parade. The social network cuts across the elite social actors in all these South Texas locations.

Moreover, all of these fiestas—Buccaneer Days, Charro Days, Fiesta San Antonio—have similar elements and ostentatious displays of wealth and power as the elites are the obvious willing performers in the spectacle.[3] Not unlike the Passion Play in Oberammergau,

Germany, where the entire town participates in one way or another in the execution of the play, the entire community is affected by the fiesta, and it becomes a communal celebration that involves various sectors of the town's population. The social and economic aspects of the fiesta notwithstanding, invariably the fiesta affects its citizens on a personal level as well. Thus, as Elaine Peña (2020, 129) states, "border enactments," a phrase she coins for the spectacles, are not specific to Laredo. In her book Peña shows that the fiesta is embedded in the community's social, economic, and political life, and that indeed, by studying the phenomenon in Laredo, we can be more informed as we deal with the challenges of border or transnational issues. I posit that it is also why we can point to the settler colonialist nature of the fiesta in Laredo. Below I discuss the Pocahontas Pageant from this perspective and explore the curious contradiction of a celebration of Indigenous identity as part of the celebration of colonial actors such as Washington, both the historical figure and what such a foundational figure represents to a colonized people. Perhaps one of the most egregious examples of the celebration's appropriation exists in the Pocahontas Pageant. Originally, the young woman selected to represent the Indigenous woman Pocahontas, who has no relation whatsoever to Laredo, was of a distinct class and social standing in the community (figs. 3.1, 3.2, 3.3). By the 1980s, when the pageant and selection of the young woman shifted to what are jokingly called Las Pokies, representatives from the local high schools competed along with the daughters of the Pocahontas Council for the title (fig. 3.4).

The economic impact of the GWBC cuts across all levels of society, from the individual vendor of balloons or of water bottles to the hospitality industry that relies on sold-out hotel capacity and full restaurants during the fiesta. As I have observed in studying fiestas in Spain and Mexico, the town's sons and daughters who have moved away return for the community's annual fiesta. As in other celebrations, tourists are drawn to the fiesta, often spurred by a publicity campaign aimed at bringing tourism to the town. From the north and the south, visitors are drawn to the Laredo celebration, where

Fig. 3.3 Carlotta Rogers Warwick and Victor Sauvignet, Laredo, Texas. This photo is unusual because in most instances, the Princess Pocahontas and her escort ride horses in the parade. Dated February 22, 1916. Courtesy of the Webb County Heritage Society.

they can attend concerts featuring Tejano and country-western bands as well as frolic and enjoy the carnival at the county fairgrounds, the various parades, and a number of free events like the fireworks display or the Air Force airshow. The latter is perhaps a holdover of the times when Laredo Air Force Base was fully integrated into Laredo society and where many Laredoans were employed. The military has always been a part of the parade, with marching bands from all branches of the military as well as units from Mexican military battalions participating with the distinctive trumpet and drum corps, leading me to ponder why and what impact it has had on the community to witness the military power represented in post– World War II displays of strength versus today when the military presence is limited. For instance, no longer are the marching bands of the branches of the military participating.

In 2020 the fiesta happened despite concern about the spread of the Coronavirus, as the confinement didn't come until March;

Fig. 3.4 The first Pocahontas selected by the newly formed Pocahontas Council was Roxy Rios, representing Martin High School in 1981. Photo courtesy of Roxy Rios.

in 2021 all events were canceled, but for 2022 things were pretty much back to normal. The high school seniors participating in the various events leading up to and during the Colonial Ball and the Grand Parade once again debuted at the Colonial Ball and rode the elaborate floats, the young women showing off their creative footwear as the crowds shouted, "Show me your shoes." In 2022 one of my grandnephews escorted a young debutante at the gala and rode in one of the floats in the parade, following his paternal family's continued participation in the fiesta. Over the years several of my

Fig. 3.5 In 1964 Governor John Connally was Señor Internacional at the Washington's Birthday Celebration. His arm is in a sling, as he was injured during the assassination of President John F. Kennedy in Dallas, Texas, a few months earlier. That year Honoré Ligarde portrayed George and María Luisa Rangel Kahn was Martha Washington. Courtesy of the Webb County Heritage Society.

siblings, nieces, nephews, grandnieces, grandnephews, and other family members have participated in the parades through their high school dance troupes, as cheerleaders, or as participants on parade floats. No one of my immediate family had participated as part of the WBCA or the Society of Martha Washington (SMW).

In 2022, once more, as it had almost uninterruptedly for 123 years, Laredo was decked out in red-white-and-blue banners as it hosted visitors from near and far, including Nancy Pelosi, who spoke at the International Bridge Ceremony before the parade and was honored by the local LULAC council as Señora Internacional at its gala. The ongoing history of the fiesta shows the influence of current events and the necessary adaptations to current realities. During the wars we see more military presence, and in 1964, Texas Governor John Connally, his arm in a sling, reminded onlookers of the not-too-distant assassination of President John Kennedy in November 1963.

A Matter of Place and Space

As the previous chapters demonstrate, a fiesta happens in context and involves a number of people directly or indirectly. A celebration's public display happens in context and for a reason. Almost as important as to why the fiestas happen is the question of where they happen. Obviously, the border spaces where these fiestas occur mark the kind and degree of spectacle they take on. The matachines and quinceañeras occur in particular and often specific spaces: for los Matachines de la Santa Cruz, it is the Barrio de la Ladrillera, now more commonly referred to as Barrio de la Santa Cruz, on the banks of the Rio Grande on the west side of Laredo. In the case of quinceañeras, it is the particular church that the family frequents and in the *salón*, or party place, that they choose for the celebration; while in previous times, the celebration happened at home, as was the case with my fiesta, more and more, especially in the late twentieth century, the fiesta moved from private homes to public rented spaces, so that *el salón* becomes the space where weddings and other life-cycle celebrations occur. Using a wider lens, we see that the broader cultural context for all three events that are the subject of this book is the US-Mexico borderlands—more specifically Texas and Tamaulipas— and the nepantla existence along that border (Anzaldúa 2002). But we must remain vigilant about just what that border signifies. Leslie Bary (2021, 63) warns against idealizing that in-between space and notes that "we are not all *mestizos* now. Some choose to enter the borderlands, but others are irrevocably there, whether they like it or not." For Laredoans and *nuevolaredenses*, the inhabitants of the two communities—Laredo and Nuevo Laredo—these fiestas, these cultural expressions, remain rooted in the historical and social reality of the land, of the piece of territory that was rent apart in 1848. The fact that they happen in one geographical space we can easily identify as the border belies the fact that these celebrations happen in such different cultural spaces and for vastly different reasons.

The GWBC in Laredo, Texas, was first organized by the fraternal organization, the Order of Red Men Yaqui Tribe #59 in the nineteenth century. As noted earlier, there had been a celebration in 1870, but for all intents and purposes, it is the 1898 celebration that is recognized as the foundational event. Young notes that the group had first considered a celebration honoring Lincoln, who is held in high esteem by Mexico and Mexicans, but he claims that the racist and southern sympathizers no doubt opposed such a selection so that the group ultimately settled on Washington as the less politically controversial figure, and someone everyone could get behind.

I have been presenting and giving lectures on the event, not just in my classes but also at professional meetings, for well over a decade, and I have always insisted that the founders of the IORM were intent on Americanizing the Mexican population, an assertion supported by various scholars and the event itself and its surround. The headline on February 22, 1898, in the *Laredo Daily Times,* "Veni, Vidi, Yaqui— Red Men Are Rustlers and Doing Grand Work in Laredo: They Will Awaken Patriotism on the Border and Make Us Realize That We Live in the United States," encapsulates the reason for the border enactment of an event that never happened.

Various scholars have offered a history of the founding of the IORM Yaqui Tribe #59 and some have offered explanations for the fiesta's persistence. Elliott Young (1998) attributes the founding of the fraternal organization to the political violence that pervaded the years between 1848 and 1900; he writes:

> Even electoral contests occasionally boiled over into violence, as occurred during a deadly election riot on the streets of Laredo in 1886. The winning party's parading a mock coffin around town to represent the other party's "death" at the polls instigated a pitched battle between the two competing and political factions, the "botas" [boots] and the "guaraches" [sandals], leaving 25 dead and 40 more wounded at the end of the day. The desire to manage and control these and other similar conflicts and to promote a "modern" image of Laredo inspired a group of prominent men to organize a citywide celebration to commemorate George Washington's birthday. (53)

I became aware of and more interested in my community's history when I first heard of this battle between political parties when I was in middle school, then called junior high. I believe it was my father who told the story. The elections at the time had a new party, the Reform Party, and my father was a supporter. My Mexican-born father was politically engaged, and although he was not a citizen yet and couldn't vote, conversations at home often revolved around politics. My mother was born in the United States, but her family had been repatriated in the 1930s, along with over five hundred thousand others, including US-born citizens, according to historians.[4] She tended to stay away from politics, although I do remember her voicing support for Kennedy.

I had attended an elementary school named after the head of the founding delegation of the Escandón expedition, Don Tomás Sánchez. But no one that I recall ever told us who Tomás Sánchez was. When I was in middle school, I became more inquisitive and found out that Lamar Junior High was named after general Mirabeau B. Lamar, a soldier and a poet who served briefly as commander of Fort McIntosh in 1847.[5] By high school I knew enough to recognize that naming of

our schools and our streets signified something, although I was not yet
theorizing and critically examining the forces that were at play. It was
just an uncanny awareness that I should be paying attention to such
practices. Certainly, I didn't link the history of the GWBC to political
violence; the fiesta's origins are rarely linked to the political violence
or the severe poverty and inequality found in the community. In fact,
Peña doesn't link the events (i.e., the political encounter between the
botas and the *guaraches*) either. However, it is one more instance of
how the motivation for the celebration may be rooted in the outsiders'
view of what Laredo was and what it could become. I was not quite
conscious of the political stranglehold our community was under as
the ruling party, el Partido Viejo, dominated and controlled all aspects
of the community politic; my budding political awareness didn't
manifest itself until my twenties. I do remember thinking with pride
that there had been *botas y guaraches* who had believed so strongly
in their cause that they had engaged in battle right here, in Laredo.
But it also made me fear for my father. Ever the activist, he was at the
time deeply engaged in a union strike at the antimony smelter where
he worked.[6] The strike lasted far longer than the workers thought it
might and it was hard times, but they held fast and were able to secure
a small pay increase and safer working conditions. Nevertheless, my
fear grew as I overheard my mother express her fears to the other
women in our neighborhood whose husbands were also involved.
I was not even a teenager, but I was already politicized and aware of
the inequities that could be addressed through action and the forces
that governed our lives.

Yet it wasn't until the late sixties, when I was enrolled in
community college and working full time at Central Power and
Light Company, that I became engaged politically and more point-
edly questioned the fiesta's reason for being. In 1968 my brother's
death in Vietnam at age nineteen had deepened my commitment to
work for social justice; at that time few opportunities arose for me to
engage in antiwar protests, but I followed the marches in Austin and
elsewhere. At my job I engaged in heated discussions with coworkers

who adamantly believed in the war and who didn't understand the whole farmworker movement. In the early seventies, I joined a local political action group, Action League of Laredo; under the tutelage of Professor Stanley Green we canvassed and did intense voter registration, hoping to add voters who would support Sissy Farenthold in her campaign for governor.

During the turmoil of the sixties and seventies, the fiestas—George Washington's birthday, the quinceañeras, and the matachines—continued as if in a cocoon, a safe space in isolation from these larger forces that were shaping our world. I contend that the social glue these fiestas offered helped participants enjoy a sense of unity and stability. In a way they lent a semblance of stability by recurring year after year and by providing the populace an outlet, a way of expressing their joys in the midst of an oftentimes-difficult life. I have observed this aspect of fiestas' role in a community elsewhere. In Navarra in Spain, Basque country, during the height of the ETA (Euskadi Ta Askatasuna, a Basque separatist group), the radical terrorist group responsible for bombings in the nineties, communities continued to observe their religious and secular fiestas despite attacks on public gatherings. In some sense it was the fiestas that kept the community together despite deep divisions within families and political factions.

I turn now to a brief discussion of how historians Jerry D. Thompson and Stanley Green have written about Laredo and have documented its history. I know Green from my time as a student at what was then Laredo State University. A scholar of Mexican history, Green arrived in Laredo in 1972 to teach at the university; Thompson arrived around the same time to teach at the community college. Both have made South Texas history the center of their academic careers. Green especially has focused on the historical narrative of leading Laredo families and his Border Studies publications. Green, who was my history professor at the local university, penned a history of the celebration (1992). He consulted the extant documents and records of the GWBCA; he interviewed numerous participants to write a nuanced history of the celebration. Similarly, Jerry Thompson, who was first

Fig. 3.6 Businesses sponsor floats in the parade. For many years businessman Sam N. Johnson III sponsored a float. He rode on the Jax Beer float c. 1960 with his friends: Garza, Mary Alice Corrigan, E. H. Corrigan Jr., and Olga LaVaude. Photo taken at the corner of San Bernardo Ave. and Washington St. in front of the A. M. Bruni home. The high school marching band follows the float. Courtesy of the Webb County Heritage Society.

a history professor at what is now Laredo College and later joined the faculty at Texas A&M International University, a prolific historian and writer whose books often focus on South Texas and on Laredo, in particular, demonstrates that Laredo has been at the center of many a debate concerning the way slavery and the local politicians played the game (1986, 1991, 2011, 2015, 2017). What these historians have found can be summed up in three overarching areas: the political, historical, and cultural. In my assessment these three are intertwined, and those involved in ensuring that the fiesta happens live within political and sociocultural realms rooted in a rich history.

The Elements of Celebration

It's mid-February and Laredo, Texas, has readied for its largest community-wide fiesta; bedecked with red, white, and blue banners, stores welcome out-of-towners and locals who are ready to party. There's a buzz of excitement in the schools as children learn about the founding fathers, color portraits of Washington, and are visited by a couple of community leaders dressed as Martha and George Washington (fig. 3.5). As Washington's birthday approaches, my hometown is in full swing for the annual GWBC festivities that run for about three weeks in February, but the Society of Martha Washington (SMW) and the George Washington's Birthday Celebration Association (GWBCA) have taken all year to plan and execute every aspect of the fiesta. One can divide the celebration into three main strands that, braided together, render the fiesta into a palimpsest of political, historical, and cultural aspects undergirding the community's identity. These and other elements that make up the celebration thread together to shape a varied and brilliant tapestry of folklife genres, including music, textiles, historical reenactments, dance, and foodways. In short, the essential elements for any community festival predominate—parades, dance and music concerts, carnival rides and foods—but with a definite Mexican twist. The hybridity of culture, as García Canclini noted, exists along borders and in this case is manifested in the fiesta.[7]

As already noted, the fiesta began in the late nineteenth century and centered on a group of elites, mostly whites but also the Mexican descendants of those who had been dispossessed of their land; it has grown into a full-fledged community celebration that seeks to unite the community in one common festival space across the entire community of Laredo, Texas, and reaches across the border to Nuevo Laredo. While it may be that the IROM had both social and economic goals in establishing the fiesta, nowadays the enterprise is also a way to generate funding for nonprofit organizations like the Border Olympics and the local Crime Stoppers. From basically a one-day event with a parade to the celebration in 2022 that included at least three unofficial events—that are not listed on their website—and eighteen official events, the fiesta has grown and gained prominence in the social life of the city. The 2022 events listed in the GWBCA website ("Events— WBCA" 2022) include:

Commander's Reception Hosted by Falcon Bank
Celebration Museum (Grand Opening)
American Historical Theatre George Washington Performance
WBCA Carnival Sponsored by McDonald's of Laredo
WBCA Founding Fathers' Run 5K, 10K and Half Marathon
WBCA Pipes & Stripes Car Show Sponsored by VitalMed Urgent Care
IBC/Commerce Bank Youth Parade Under the Stars
WBCA/La Posada Hotel Welcome Luncheon
WBCA Jalapeño Festival Sponsored by La Costeña—Friday
WBCA/IGNC International Bridge Ceremony Sponsored by La Posada Hotel
Anheuser-Busch Washington's Birthday Parade
Mr. South Texas Luncheon Hosted by Texas Community Bank
WBCA Jalapeño Festival Sponsored by La Costeña—Saturday
WBCA Membership BBQ
H-E-B Fireworks Extravaganza
WBCA Carnival Sponsored by McDonald's of Laredo: McMonday
WBCA Stars & Stripes Air Show Spectacular Sponsored by Miller Lite
WBCA President's Cup Golf Tournament Sponsored by Vantage Bank

The first official event of the annual celebration, the Commander's Reception, was held on January 19, a full month before the celebration's main event, the Anheuser-Busch Washington's Birthday Parade. The last official event, the Golf Tournament, was not held until March 4. And the Menudo Bowl was rescheduled from January 22 to March 26 due to the surge in COVID cases in January of that year.

The GWBC from its origins has had numerous opportunities for gathering and celebrating that hint at political affiliation or political underpinnings. Initially it was the staging of the Boston Tea Party and then came the parade with elected officials and a visible military presence; other elements have been added subsequently, such as the abrazo ceremony on the bridge sponsored by the Pan American Round Table. It's not unusual for major policies or citywide events to be linked to the celebration; the political elements emerged early as the fiesta became the backdrop for national and even international agreements and exchanges. When Porfirio Díaz sent a marching band to participate in the parade in 1901, according to Stanley C. Green (1992), the fiesta took on an international tone. Subsequently, and as I remember in the 1950s and 60s, the Mexican participation in the parade was pronounced. Additionally, with the establishment of the abrazo, including the children's abrazo, sponsored by the local International Good Neighbor Council and the Pan American Round Table, the bonds were strengthened. According to Peña (2020, 88–91), as the political leaders from Nuevo Laredo and Laredo met in an official act, and as the delegation from Laredo participated in events in Nuevo Laredo, the transnational tenor became a significant element of the fiesta. As Peña aptly documents in her chapter on the *paso libre*, or open crossing, the abrazo event held at the critical national boundary halfway on the bridge is a telling part of the political encounters of the festival, one that has changed in recent years. The open border was no more; first the violence or the threat of violence and later the COVID restrictions further impelled dramatic changes to the transnational activities.

In 1933 the Border Olympics was organized to display the region's athletic prowess; it has grown into an annual event drawing athletes from all over South Texas and Northern Mexico. The fundraiser and unofficial start of the GWBC that the Border Olympics organization sponsors, the Stockman's Ball, sets off the festivities.

Other events throughout the month-long celebration include something for every sector of the society, such as the Princess Pocahontas Pageant, the Colonial Ball, the Jalapeño Festival, and many others that have been added to the original fiesta, including a lowrider car show and a comedy show, Jam for George. Children get a chance to participate in the youth parade; teenagers gather with friends and hang out at the carnival, an activity that is mostly geared for children and families; most young adults will laugh at Jam for George—a comedy event where local stand-up comics join headliners from out of town—and the daughters and sons of the elites will take part in the Pocahontas Pageant or the Colonial Ball, a definite display of wealth and power, although each has a particular echelon along the social scale.[8]

Volunteers, officers, and members of SMW, along with the debutantes and their escorts, work for an entire year, during which they attend numerous social events and prepare for the fiesta, culminating in the Colonial Ball following the presentation. At the presentation ball in the fall, the debs, the young women daughters of the members of the SMW (commonly referred to as "las Marthas"), don formal white gowns and are escorted by their fathers. They enter individually and promenade around the dance floor. A seated dinner followed by live-music dance serves as the evening's entertainment. The big event, the Colonial Pageant and Ball, captured by Cristina Ibarra in her film, *Las Marthas* (2014), is under the coordination of the SMW and involves numerous volunteers. At this culminating event, the debs with their escorts are presented along with a prominent couple who portray Martha and George Washington (fig. 3.8).

I want to take a few paragraphs to discuss the Princess Pocahontas Pageant, as it is, in my view, a problematic representation and laden with issues. It too commemorates an event that never happened—in this case a reenactment of a mock battle between the townspeople and the Indigenous. At the end peace is achieved and Princess Pocahontas receives the keys to the city at a ceremony during the International Parade. I have described the matachines de la Santa Cruz and their faith belief in the Holy Cross as well as their fiesta to honor the Holy Cross on May 3. Despite the fact that the tradition is obviously based in Indigenous practices, they do not readily claim indigeneity. In a chapter in a book on identity, I discuss the matachines and their performance of indigeneity (Cantú 2012). I also discuss the relationship between the GWBC and the matachines in "*Dos Mundos*: Two Celebrations in Laredo, Texas—Los Matachines de la Santa Cruz and the Pocahontas Pageant of the George Washington's Birthday Celebration," a chapter in a book on cultural production (2011).

The performance of indigeneity in the Pocahontas Pageant is vastly different both in intent and in tone. The Princess Pocahontas Council stages a Princess Pocahontas Pageant on Saturday a week before the Colonial Pageant and Ball. Similar to the GWBC Colonial Ball celebrating Washington's birthday, the pageant includes an event that is wholly imagined; the battle includes a pageant with a narrative that describes the reason the various tribes have come together. In early celebrations the peaceful resolution included a peace pipe, a symbol of the group's friendship. The symbolic event of handing the keys to the city to Pocahontas happens at the parade as the mayor hands the young woman portraying Pocahontas a large symbolic key. Each year the Pocahontas Council creates a narrative around Native American symbols and tribes that for the most part are not in any way linked to the local Indigenous groups and do not have a historical connection to the land. Instead, they draw from various Indigenous groups from the north and the northeast.

The cultural impact of the celebration harkens back to an attempt to impose a US identity onto a truly historically Mexican community; perhaps the group that established the Pocahontas Council was in some ways resisting the erasure of the Indigenous by the settler colonialism that pervaded and pervades the ethos of Laredo. Still, in some ways the group falls into a similar trap by idealizing and recreating events that never happened; by reenacting an imagined event and thereby rendering invisible the original Indigenous groups of the area, the fiesta is complicit in the denial of the Indigenous legacy of the area.

If the Pocahontas Pageant was intended as a counternarrative to the settler colonialism of the GWBC narrative, then we can argue that there's been, if not outright resistance, at least some questioning of the celebration's aim. Cordelia Barrera, in her book *The Haunted Southwest:*

Towards an Ethics of Place in Borderlands Literature (2022), explores the contradictions found in the fiesta as she writes of the "bordered frontier" and defines that intertwining of the imagined and mythological frontier of the southwest imaginary with the very real geopolitical border and what happens there. The most salient and perhaps most egregious aspects of the Pocahontas Pageant's role within the GWBC fiesta is the fact that the real Indigenous—indeed the ancestors of many of the young people participating in the event—are not given a voice, nor are they represented. In a different project, I intend to go through all the program books to find traces or allusions to local Indigenous groups, as I have not observed any such mention in the ones I have witnessed. For now, I limit my comments to the ways that the GWBC has subsumed and made even this event a part of the larger fiesta. I now turn to two contests that are tied to food: the Menudo Bowl Cook-Off and the Jalapeño Eating Contest that is part of the Jalapeño Festival.

Foodways Contests

As in most fiestas, food plays an important role. For the quinceañeras the festive meal is traditionally the red chile delicacy, mole, or often in South Texas, brisket or other such festive food. Of course, there's also a birthday cake and a special drink. For the matachines the meal varies according to the resources and who is in charge of the preparation: mole, brisket, or simply rice, beans, and some kind of protein— either chicken or beef. Similarly, for the GWBC the food tends to fit the occasion, and at the carnival, for instance, one can enjoy the usual kettle corn, cotton candy, and funnel cakes found in country fairs and festivals. But for the GWBC, two other foods, not generally for regular consumption, are found in food-preparation contests. Such contests are common in South Texas; in fact, I served as a judge at a brisket cook-off in Kingsville, Texas, in the heart of cattle country on homecoming weekend at Texas A&M University–Kingsville. Such cooking contests are stratified and demonstrate the community's value on certain regional foodways.

The Menudo Bowl Cook-Off

Unlike the Stockman's Ball that began in the very early days of the GWBC fiesta, the two food events I discuss here are fairly recent additions. For twenty-six years, the Menudo Bowl Cook Off has been drawing throngs of Laredoans and South Texans to taste and judge the area's best menudo, a delicacy made with beef tripe and spicy red chiles and eaten with condiments like onion, cilantro, oregano, and turnips. The dish is not an easy one to fix and requires hours of preparation and cooking. My father's recipe—yes, for some reason, most of the cooks are male—took him a good chunk of time as he cleaned and prepared the tripe, mixed the spices, and then cooked the stew over low heat for hours. I must confess that I do like the taste, and even when I was vegetarian I would cheat by spooning a few kernels of hominy from the broth to get the delicious taste if not the meat. It's not a dish for everyone, and I have known many who cannot stand the smell of the menudo cooking, much less the texture of biting into the piece of tripe. Others prefer to eat the hominy and leave the meat alone—as I just described I would do. But my eating predilections can wait for another time. Suffice it to say that the various cooks who have set up booths at the Webb County Fairgrounds bring their already-cooked menudo in large pots. They ladle the menudo into Styrofoam bowls for the judges and hope that theirs will appeal to all of them. Each year the event kicks off the GWBC fiesta. It is a fundraiser, as are many other events.

In 2022 the Menudo Bowl Cook-Off, the Menudo Bowl for short, was postponed from January 22 to March 26 due to the COVID surge that occurred in Laredo in early January ("Laredo's 2022 Menudo Bowl Postponed" 2022). This foodways event that determines who cooks the best menudo in town raises around $75,000 for the Laredo Crime Stoppers organization.[9] The Menudo Bowl organization, usually comprised of volunteers, registers participants and charges for attendance; in addition to generating the prize money, the organization raises operating funds so Laredo Crime Stoppers can pay off the tipsters who provide information leading to arrests. The Menudo Bowl is an all-day event held at the Webb County Fairgrounds. The highlight of the event is the award for the best menudo. Individuals and restaurants compete. The timing of the event is what makes it part of the fiesta activities, although it is not an official event of GWBCA. Judges are sometimes solicited from local chefs but often they are also brought in from out of town. In 2022 judges included local restaurateur Luis Antonio Lara, owner of El Puesto Taqueria & Cantina; Valeria Contreras, of a local coffee shop, Caffe Dolce; Mariajose Velásquez, local foodie and influencer; Nahum Eli and Yahaira Hernández of Sal y Limón Snack; Raul and Karina Gallegos, owners of Barrio de Brazil; and Anita Guerra of Tremendo Taco.

The cook-off also involves the selection of a young woman to be Miss Laredo Crime Stoppers at a staged pageant, and the day ends with the evening's pro wrestling matches. All in all, the January event brings out those ready to gather and listen to Tejano and conjunto music and eat hearty menudo and other delicacies. The judges award three prizes in open division category as follows: first place wins $1000; second place, $750; and third place, $500. All three get a trophy as well. The people's choice wins $300 and a trophy.

As I mentioned earlier, it is mostly men who compete (and win). Contestants prepare for weeks before the event and guard their secret recipes. Restaurants send their best chefs to compete, and the winner can boast that their menudo was deemed the best, at least for a year, until the next cook-off happens. Individuals also compete in the open category and take great pride in having their savory dish achieve the title of the best menudo. I have known a few men who almost came to blows because of the judges' decision. The heated (pun intended) contest brings professionals and amateurs to compete for the title of the best menudo. The event is fun and there's an excitement in the air as judges savor the various beef tripe stews. Menudo is known to be a cure for hangovers and, given the fiesta's many late-night events where indubitably people have too much to drink, it is an important component of the celebration. Now, the Jalapeño Festival has also been around for decades, but unlike the Menudo Cook-Off, it is sponsored by a commercial enterprise, La Costeña.[10]

Jalapeño Festival

The Jalapeño Festival is embedded into the GWBC festivities and includes three contests: El Grito contest, the Jalapeño Eating contest, and the Miss Jalapeño beauty pageant. When I first attended, there was no Grito contest; that has been added, to the delight of many in the audience. Briefly, the contest rewards the person whom the judges deem delivers the best "Grito"—a kind of vocal performance of a yell or scream that accompanies Mexican ranchera songs. The second contest is self-explanatory: contestants are seated at a long table and are timed to see who can eat the most peppers in a given time frame. And the third, as in Ms. Crime Stoppers, the Miss Jalapeño winner is selected from a cadre of young women through a selection committee. She is usually dressed in green, and at one event I attended she was in fact wearing a bikini while encased in a huge jalapeño contraption. Both Miss Laredo Crime Stoppers and Miss Jalapeño get to ride a float or a special entry car in Saturday's parade.

In 2021 and 2022, with some restrictions, the fiesta went ahead as planned, and the Jalapeño Festival with its music, food, and contests was no exception. Quoted in a *Laredo Morning Times* online article, Armando Angeles expressed what many in the community were feeling: "The fact that the bridges are now opened and COVID is almost gone means that now my family can come and listen to this beautiful music." He was further quoted as saying, "You don't know how much I miss doing things with my brothers and sisters from Nuevo Laredo, and this is something that we can finally do together in efforts to get this accomplished" (Vela 2021). His words express the transnationality of the celebration and how much the community that may be divided on some level is still united as family ties reach across the Rio Grande.

The Jalapeño Eating Contest and the Menudo Cook-Off are only two foodways events that happen as part of the GWBCA fiesta. The Colonial Pageant Ball and the Pocahontas Pageant showcase the young people—daughters and sons of the elites in town—and remain restrictive to some degree, due to the price of attending the events, while the food contests seem to be aimed at a general audience and remain accessible to anyone, with tickets sold at a more modest price.

Fireworks

The festival essentials—parades, music concerts, fireworks, and the carnival rides—are part of the communal memory of those of us who grew up in Laredo and form the backdrop of life. Many of us didn't question the premise or the anachronism of such a celebration but instead, as in many communities, just went along and participated unquestioningly.

In the 1950s of my youth, we gathered at the old grounds west of Martin High School bordered by San Bernardo and Santa Maria Avenues; the stands had been set up for the fireworks in the area where we now find the Laredo Civic Center and a municipal swimming pool. The sounds, smells of *la pólvora*, and the night sky coming alive with brilliant and colorful rockets that shot up and burst, raining stars that seemed to descend upon our heads, remains imprinted in my mind, as does the closing display of outlines of George Washington and of patriotic red, white, and blue flags on either side of the portrait that was lit up at the conclusion of the pyrotechnic display. Peña (2020) describes a fireworks display that sounds surprisingly similar to the one I witnessed as a child in the 1950s, but *la pólvora* is no longer what it used to be; in fact, I haven't heard anyone call it that in some years. Although it remains on the schedule, it is no longer held at the outset to start the festivities but at the conclusion, on Sunday evening. Moreover, the location has been moved east of town to the Webb County Fairgrounds.

Remembering a Past That Never Was

One can imagine that the first family celebrated Washington's birthday, but there is no evidence of a birthday party hosted by Martha anywhere, and even if there were, it would have been held on the East Coast, at Mt. Vernon, no doubt, not in Laredo. The celebration commemorates an imagined and constructed event in our nation's history. We might question the presumption of the organizers in the nineteenth century and arrive at a quick answer: politics and economics. I submit that the fiesta fits both beautifully, as it happens between the Christmas and Easter festivities; moreover, as a secular festival, all sectors of society are potential participants. It being a ranching culture, the winter is an excellent time to come together without disrupting the ranching traditions of early spring or autumn, when cowboys and ranch folk are busy with the task of cattle ranching. In fact, the first official event of the celebration is the Stockman's Ball, a celebration that features a country-western performer and a lively dance. It is a self-selected audience that dresses in their finest western wear and comes out to enjoy the music and to dance a Cotton-Eye-Joe or a Texas two-step.

The community celebration has something for everyone, from the Jam for George comedy event that one of my nephews was instrumental in establishing—also called Jamming with George at one time—to the Colonial Ball, where my grandnephew donned colonial era dress to escort one of the Marthas.

As a child I remember going to the parade and the carnival (fig. 3.6). As a teen it was pure joy to meet other teenagers in town for the celebration and stroll around the carnival grounds. And the parade! What a thrill to be a part of it. There is a picture of me on a convertible, participating in the parade as a member of a high school group, the Pan American Student Forum. Later, as a young adult, working as a clerk at the local utilities' office, I went with friends to the Jalapeño Festival, where I first heard a very young Selena Quintanilla belt out her songs. As I grew more critical and understood the rationale for the celebration, I protested the bridge ceremony. One such protest occurred in 1998, along with writer Sandra Cisneros and others who wanted to stage some sort of countercelebration on the bank of the river. Not surprisingly, amid the hullabaloo on the bridge with dignitaries and the Grand Parade, our protest went unnoticed.

I now understand it a bit better but am still conflicted about the way the city celebrates a mostly alien and settler colonialist event that has so little to do with our beleaguered community that has suffered from militarized occupation off and on since its founding in 1755. Moreover, in recent years the militarized zone that the border has become has been shown more and more at the celebration. In the upcoming fiesta, it is the Border Patrol and the Texas Rangers that will serve as parade marshals for the IBC/Commerce Bank Youth Parade Under the Stars and the Anheuser-Busch Washington's Birthday Parade, respectively. What happens next? In my view, we continue. Laredo continues to celebrate and to engage in a most obvious and blatant performance of settler colonialism that reinstates our status as outsiders while claiming to affirm our insider status as US citizens. We are indeed strangers in our own land. The GWBCA and the SMW will continue as the daughters and sons of the current leadership emerge to take on leadership roles and to honor the legacy of their ancestors.

Afterword

As I write this in 2023, a month after the fiesta, I reminisce and think back to last summer when I wrote: In the summer of 2022 plans were well underway for the 2023 events; the principal players had been picked and the new inductees into the board of directors had been elected. The dates had been set: January 19–February 26, 2023. Undoubtedly the community would come out and celebrate as it has for 125 years. My grandniece would be among the debutantes attending the innumerable receptions and events leading up to the Colonial Ball where she, as her paternal grandmother and aunts did during their time, would be making her bow, dressed as they were in an elaborate simulacrum of an eighteenth-century dress, albeit much heavier and more a costume that exaggerates the performance than anything Martha Washington or her contemporaries ever wore. But authenticity is not the point. Neither is the fact that the Spanish settlers who first came to this land and who are my grandniece's ancestors would've been opposed to the gesture and aghast at the allegiance given to who they would consider barbaric enemies. The defeat of the Spanish Armada two centuries earlier had not been forgotten, and the Spanish who made their way to the Americas brought with them that distrust of the British just as they brought— in my estimation—a desire for conquest that went beyond proselytizing and gaining converts to the faith; after all, Spain was by now Catholic and the United States was not. They brought a hunger for land and for conquest, marrying church and military to achieve that goal. The first to arrive and the later ones established a world to replicate as much as they could the one they left behind. But they couldn't resist the influence of those they came in contact with and with whom they soon intermarried. The encounters of Cabeza de Vaca in this very region of South Texas attest to the ways our Indigenous ancestors interacted with the newcomers. Reading his account, we can see who were the real Indigenous groups in the area, not the ones imagined by the Princess Pocahontas Council. In like manner we can recall the Spanish and their descendants, like our great-grandparents and grandparents, who survived despite tremendous odds, including health and the geographical catastrophes of their time. Like them, we too survive. We create mechanisms to allow our own survival and to ensure our memory remains true to them. Fiestas achieve that to a degree, for we find solace in the repetition, in the replication, in the patterning of time that they offer.

The influx of Anglo settlers similarly impacted the Spanish and mestizo community. The settler colonialism that Laredoans practice and live under cannot be overlooked, yet it must be problematized and complicated by the reality of a lived experience along a border that creates the land/space where such events happen. It is not one but two colonizing powers that exercise power and impose a cultural colonization that renders us unwittingly the actors in a scene that repeats itself as if in a loop from generation to generation. The single elements may change, but the structure of the systemic frame does not. The church and the state govern the actions or inactions of individuals who have learned to survive. The concept of power and coloniality, as Quijano (1991, 2001/2002) notes, occurs in relation to exploitation and domination. According to him, "The four basic areas of human existence: sex, labor, collective authority and subjectivity/intersubjectivity, their resources and products" are at the root of the colonial enterprise (2001/2002, 1). But it is this display of power that the fiestas enact and reinforce within the performance. As performative as the various aspects and elements of the fiesta are, we cannot ignore that they serve a strong purpose at the sociopolitical level. In addition to lending a cohesion to the social fabric, I submit that the fiesta perhaps more importantly asserts the community's identity in a binational and bicultural space.

Joe S. Graham, when speaking of material culture claimed, "First to survive, the tradition must remain an integral part of some important aspect of life. Second, the craft must continue to serve its utilitarian function at least as effectively as its popular culture counterpart. And third, it must continue to meet the aesthetic demands of the people who maintain the tradition, doing so in a way which its popular-culture counterpart cannot" (1992, 10). I posit that the same goes for performance and ritual and, in this case, fiestas. They survive because they remain an "integral part" of the community's social life. Moreover, it continues to serve a function—in this case, it is not vis-à-vis popular culture; in fact, it has in some ways become a hybrid of tradition and popular culture by adding or subsuming elements such as the El Grito or Jalapeño Eating Contests.

I want to caution readers lest the expectation is that this book is an excoriation of the events I am writing about. That is not it at all. By questioning, by thinking about what and why we do things like celebrate a coming of age, or a religious feast, or an imagined event, I do not imply that we should judge it to be wrong or even misguided, as some readers may be wont to do. No. Instead I would like to offer a glimpse into these celebrations, these fiestas that my hometown embraces and relishes and whereby we find our identity with a sense of love and loyalty. Were it not for these fiestas, we would not be who we are. All communities need their fiestas, and we have ours.

Good or bad, it is not for me to judge but only to lay out and present them as I see them. I urge us to think of why they occur and what they mean, what it means that they occur at all. Ultimately, the ancestors who have lived and have come before us left us a legacy, and whether we embrace it or not, we cannot deny that they were establishing mechanisms for survival on various levels. With sincere intentions and with a sentipensante approach, I offer this brief view of these three fiestas as a way to get to know my community, or at least the various parts of the community that draws strength and are nourished by the fiestas.

It is February 2023, only a couple of days before the big weekend of the GWBC, and we are reminded that COVID, while not the threat it was during the pandemic, is still among us. My nephew who was supposed to attend the GWBC to see his niece presented at the Society of Martha Washington's Presentation Ball has tested positive and will miss it. No doubt other families are also dealing with similar situations; quinceañeras canceled or greatly reduced, as happened with the matachines in May. But the fiestas survive and carry on. I hope to participate and see my grandniece be presented and celebrate her and all her accomplishments as she readies for high school graduation and goes on to college. This particular grandniece didn't have a quinceañera, and the GWBC, it seems to me, functions similarly—a presentation where she wore a white formal gown and danced with her father and with her escort, the same young man who will be her escort at the GWBCA Presentation Ball on Friday night and ride at her side on the float at the Grand Parade on Saturday morning.

This weekend, it is not likely that many young women will celebrate their quinceañera in Laredo, as it would conflict with the GWBC. But, undoubtedly, the following weekend Instagram and Facebook posts will once again feature families celebrating quinceañeras, and the *Laredo Morning Times* will have photos of young women in their quinceañera dresses.

While residents bemoan the fact that the community remains without access to what much of the rest of the country enjoys, such as a

PBS radio station or even certain chain restaurants like P. F. Chang's, few point to the dire needs of a large portion of the population that remains largely marginalized, save some local celebrities who have emerged. The ever-needy food bank and the high rate of students who qualify for financial assistance, not to mention the high number of migrants who gain asylum hearings and stay glutting the Catholic Charities services, are testament to the needs in the community, contrasting with such lavish display of wealth as can be seen in the GWBCA events. But some resistance exists. One such is muckraker Priscilla Villarreal Treviño, a.k.a. la GordiLoca, a one-woman dynamo whose social media following surpasses that of the local newspaper. Offending many in the community with what some call her "foul mouth," she reports via Facebook livestream what is going on in the community, often calling politicians and other power brokers to task. The granddaughter of one of my mother's *comadres*, she has emerged as a powerhouse (Tyx 2019).[11]

The impact of the local higher education institutions cannot be overemphasized, as the educational level has increased over-whelmingly since I first registered for classes over fifty years ago at what is now Texas A&M International University. The commu-nity's many problems are exacerbated by the poverty rate and the concomitant social effects. Ninety-five percent of the population is of Mexican origin, and the language of the community remains Spanish; although there has been an increase in the high school grad-uation rates since I graduated in 1965, young people still go into the military or find low-paying jobs locally. According to the informa-tion shared at the presentation of the nine 2023 debutantes and their escorts, many of them were planning on going on to college at Texas A&M University in College Station or the University of Texas in Austin or San Antonio.

In 2023 my grandniece, one of nine debutantes, is what is called a "legacy" participant, as her paternal family has been involved in the celebration for generations, as have the families of the couple

who portrayed George and Martha Washington: Joe Palacios and
Christie Alexander. I attended the pageant and ball and, of course,
the International Parade. I observed with interest the ways that the
fiesta ritualistically repeats certain elements, but I also observed the
changes. The Pokies and the Marthas were still front and center as
the crowds waited with anticipation, but there were some changes.
Not surprisingly, interspersed along with to-be-expected high school
bands and dance teams, were numerous commercial floats sponsored by local businesses, including one for a bail bond company
with an elaborately decorated float that included a makeshift jail cell
with someone in it. Gone were the military bands or the Clydesdale
horses; instead, various policing units in town marched, in some cases
alongside floats decorated with their insignia. Among them were the
Customs and Border Protection, the Laredo Police Department, the
Webb County judge and sheriff, and constables who rode horseback.
The criminal justice agencies that patrol the border and our community. Also a surprise for me was the inclusion of a key figure in our
community, Bishop James A. Tamayo, DD, who assumed the role
of bishop for the newly formed Diocese of Laredo at San Agustin
Cathedral in 2000 (fig. 3.7).

As the parade wound down and people started leaving, I imagined
what the many young children would remember. The little girl atop
her father's shoulders reminded me of my own privileged spot those
many years ago, and the young boys and girls running up to the horses
or to the floats to touch them and to see if they would be rewarded
with a string of beads or a lollipop from those in the parade brought
back memories as well. I didn't go to the Jalapeño Festival or any of
the other parts of the fiesta. One nephew, who is a standup comedian
and a founder of the Jam for George, was involved, as were many
other relatives: a niece who is the head cheerleader for her high school
cheer squad marched and performed. My brother-in-law, a former
police officer who for over twenty years was in the honor guard leading the parade, stood by quietly observing it all, immersed no doubt

Fig. 3.7 Bishop of the Diocese of Laredo, Most Reverend James A. Tamayo, DD, in the parade in 2023. Photo by Norma E. Cantú.

in his own memories of all those years. I asked dozens of people what their earliest memories of the fiesta were, and invariably the parade and the carnival emerged. But the fireworks, the Jalapeño Festival, and the bridge ceremony also came up.

Fig. 3. 8 Ariana Botello, debutante at the Society of Martha Washington Debutante Ball in February 2023. Her paternal grandmother and her aunts have been part of the celebration for decades. Courtesy of Ariana Botello.

The fiestas—matachines, quinceañeras, and the GWBC—will continue, and my beloved Laredo will continue to suffer the vicissitudes of being a border city with all the opportunities for success and growth, along with the challenges of being the largest inland port with over five thousand freight trucks crossing from Mexico, loaded with goods going north. The fiestas remain as reminders of our past and a testament to the present as well as a hope for the future. They are a reminder that our community is indeed unique and perhaps not exceptional, but certainly unforgettable.

Conclusion

Some Theoretical Musings in the Form of a Coda

A s I conclude this book and my writing about the three celebrations that I have known all of my life, I can't help but dwell on
theoretical leanings and observations that may answer my questions
about why Laredo still has these fiestas while others have gone by
the wayside and remain forgotten. However critical that question is,
in some way the real question is, What does it mean that we keep
celebrating fiestas, keep coming together—in our community, our
families, our town—to celebrate and communally honor tradition?

When I read Elliott Young's article, "Red Men, Princess Pocahontas,
and George Washington: Harmonizing Race Relations in Laredo at the
Turn of the Century" published in *The Western Historical Quarterly* in
1998, I was intrigued by his argument that dimension of the celebration
revealed political and social information about the community's past
and its current political climate. It was then that I thought I should
write about the fiestas in my community of Laredo, Texas, and how
from an insider's perspective it is more than just that. All these years,
the idea has been but a dream until now. The intricate social relations
that happen in Laredo and in many border communities are yet to

be examined. In social engagement theory, as scholars like Aida Hurtado (1997) have laid out, it is not necessarily assimilation that occurs to survive the oppressions of late capitalism, but the reliance and *movidas*[1] of subjects seeking to retain their identity and the mores of their cultural group. The social customs surrounding the fiestas bind the community together; the fiestas in turn sustain the continued traditional practices of the community and thus affirm identity.

Coloniality and Decoloniality

I would be remiss if I did not point out and note how in all three fiestas at the center of this book, we can discern the vestiges or residue of the colonial project in South Texas, doubly so, in fact; first we find the colonizing Spanish over the Indigenous and secondly the colonizing Anglo or United Statesian project over the Mexican-origin, mestizo, and the Indigenous who remained in the town in 1848 at the time of the signing of the Treaty of Guadalupe Hidalgo. While my focus is not on this obvious question of coloniality in these celebrations, I cannot ignore the blatant settler colonialism we find in Laredo that is manifested through the fiestas. It would be a different project to dig deeper into this settler colonialism and into decolonial *movidas* and to explore the many ways the community engages in acts of resistance. In the case of the three fiestas in Laredo, I point to certain *movidas* that function similarly as a resistance against the colonizing impetus of both Spanish and Anglo forces, including the linguistic and cultural stirrups that nudge the horse forward. Suffice it to say that by acknowledging and underscoring the significance of the material reality that settler colonialism harbors, I am providing an opening for other scholars to perform such analyses. I provide a perfunctory exploration of such an analysis.

Scholars who have gleaned that coloniality deeply pervades society (Mignolo 2000; Quijano 2001/2002; Lugones 2007, 2010) point to geopolitics, race, gender, and power differentials as manifestations of the colonial project. The GWBC's history in our community underscores the historical grounding but also the dissonance of having a performance of a historical event that is on multiple levels at odds with the majority of the population and the community but in which the majority of its denizens participate and celebrate. Laredo, I have heard said over and over, is different. How so? I ask, and invariably people point to the diversity of our community that has embraced newcomers from its founding in 1755 to the present.[2] The foundational narrative is of the community's ability to integrate the newcomer, the stranger, into its folds.

It is no coincidence that the street names in Laredo follow a certain pattern. For a graduate class, I wrote a paper on the streets of Laredo, and I have been thinking about these streets' symbolic naming ever since. Coming up from the river, the first twelve streets are named after historical figures: Zaragoza, Grant, Iturbide, Lincoln, Hidalgo, Farragut, Matamoros, Houston, Victoria, Washington, Moctezuma. Actually, the first street is Water Street; it runs along the riverbank. After Moctezuma Street, the street names follow a different pattern, as it appears that it is the names of mayors that follow, including Coke, Benavides, Garcia, Callaghan, and Garza. The intersecting avenues are the typical Main and Convent, but it is quite revealing that the others are names of saints: Santa Rita, Santa Cleotilde, San Bernardo, San Agustin, Santa Ursula, San Dario, San Francisco, and San Eduardo. Obviously, such naming reflects the way the society's parameters are the military and the church. Up until the 1970s, Laredo Air Force Base was a force in the community, and it seemed natural that a military base be a strong presence in the community as it had been in the latter part of the nineteenth century when Fort McIntosh established order along the border. Indeed, some GWBCA events were held at air base venues, and up until the 1970s, many of the parade floats were assembled and stored in the old barracks at Fort McIntosh. When the base was shut down, for a brief time there seemed to be a lull as mostly local policing organizations remained; nowadays it is not only city and state agencies that monitor and police the city but also the omnipresent federal agencies like ICE whose agents roam the streets of Laredo in ever-increasing numbers. Like a panopticon, the multiple criminal (in)justice agencies and their surveillance apparatus ushered in a shift in the community's day-to-day activities in general and in the fiestas in particular.

Scholars like Chicano historian David Montejano (1987) assert that social and economic factors shaped South Texas's unique social structure. I would add that these social and economic factors are rooted in the community's celebrations that undergird the social and economic relations. We are now at the threshold of a new shift that will continue to rely on the fiestas and on the people's faith beliefs and resilience. The Matáchines will continue to hold sacred dance tradition in their enclave on the banks of the Rio Grande and the private family parties for young women turning fifteen will continue; and as long as the SMW and other organizing pillars of the fiesta continue to be fueled by economic and social desires, the GWBC will continue to entertain and provide winter respite to Laredoans and Nuevo Laredoans.

In my view the fiestas of Laredo offer a rich laboratory for study and for ontological discovery. It is my hope that scholars will continue to marvel at the phenomena and to write about and study our unique cultural expressions. Fiestas provide ground-level experiences that reflect the people's lives and Laredo's ethos of celebrating and relishing tradition. But perhaps more importantly, fiestas constitute a necessary and essential part of life for the citizens of Laredo, a part of the very essence of the community's identity. What more can one ask of events that have been around for more than a century in a community with roots that go back more than three hundred years? ¡Qué vivan las fiestas!

Endnotes

Notes for Introduction

1. For a discussion of Anzaldúa's *autohistoria-teoría*, see Kakali Bhattacharya's (2020) article "Autohistoria-teoría: Merging Self, Culture, Community, Spirit, and Theory."
2. The photocopy of that particular text can be found at the Nettie Lee Benson Collection at the University of Texas at Austin Library.
3. At the time, the 1950s, Mexican-origin children were punished physically for speaking Spanish; I was 6 years old and I remember the shame and embarrassment, not to mention the pain, of being hit by our teacher with a ruler for speaking Spanish. It is no wonder that many of us chose not to teach our children Spanish and many of us forgot the language. For a documentary that explores the racism that existed at the time, see Rudy Luna and Enrique Alemán's documentary, *Stolen Education* (2013).
4. For a discussion of how the apparently commonplace chat, or *plática*, can be a methodological strategy for scholars to gather information, see Cindy O. Fierros and Dolores Delgado Bernal (2016).
5. See Alejandro Valderas's discussion of the Ramo de Navidad in León (2009)
6. Cherríe Moraga discusses the concept of "making familia from scratch" (1986, 58) in a different context and in reference to the LGBTQ community in *This Bridge Called My Back: Writings by Radical Women of Color* (2002).
7. See Ruth Behar's *The Vulnerable Observer: Anthropology that Breaks the Heart* (1996) for a discussion of a "humanistic anthropology" that in a way practices a sentipensante methodology.

Notes for Chapter 1

1. Author's translation.
2. *Mestizaje* has been the subject of various scholarly studies; in this context it basically refers to the interweaving of more than one cultural group. In the case of the matachines, we can discern the influences from Spanish and Indigenous traditions. See Néstor Medina (2009) for an insightful discussion of *mestizaje* within the Catholic Church.
3. *Mexica* is the term that the Indigenous inhabitants of Tenochtitlan and Tlatelolco used historically to refer to themselves. The term *Aztec* (or *Azteca*) designates a person from the *Mexica*'s ancestral homeland of Aztlan.
4. See Max Harris's "The Return of Moctezuma: Oaxaca's 'Danza de La Pluma' and New Mexico's 'Danza de Los Matachines'" (1997) for a discussion of matachines in New Mexico and in Oaxaca.
5. For a discussion of the dances in Tlaxcala during the late sixteenth century, see Harris 2000 (138–39, 145–47).
6. For information on the mines and the matachines and other cultural expressions there, see Josephine Worsham Garcia, *The Coal Mines* (n.d., unpublished manuscript, Laredo Public Library).
7. Every year a member of the matachines community is in charge of "dressing the cross" with flowers. Since I started documenting it, it has fallen to the Liendo family to do this. Doña Sarita was in charge until she became too elderly and passed on the task to her daughter-in-law Claudina (1930–2016), who was married to Sarita's son, Lorenzo "Tiolle" Liendo; after Claudina's passing, her sister-in-law, Carolina (1945–2020), who was married to Sarita's son Isaac Liendo, was in charge of dressing the cross. Her daughters Elodia and Carolina, as well as her son, Isaac Jr., dressed the cross in 2021. Recently, Isaac expressed interest in taking charge of the fiesta as the Ortiz brothers are older and may be getting ready to pass it on back to the Liendo family. As with

most things associated with the tradition, the Dressing of the Cross falls to a certain family that then passes on the task across generations; the Liendo family members have been dressing the Holy Cross for at least seventy-five years.

8. As noted earlier, because of COVID-19 CDC guidelines and the City of Laredo restrictions, the fiesta did not happen for two years; however, the dancing did happen, albeit in a much-reduced form. I spoke with Doña Panchita Ortiz, the matriarch of the group, the day before the fiesta in 2021, and she bemoaned the fact that the city had not allowed any gatherings of more than ten and definitely not issued them a permit for the procession to go to the church and set up the cross. Nevertheless, she informed me that a very small group would dance "el mero día de la Santa Cruz." In 2022 the fiesta was celebrated with some dancers wearing masks.

9. Information about the group and the National Heritage Fellows tribute video can be found at https://www.arts.gov/honors/heritage/los-matachines-de-la-santa-cruz-de-la-ladrillera.

Notes for Chapter 2

1. In previous work I have cited Arnold van Gennep (1960, 24) for his notions of liminality apply to the coming-of-age celebration.

2. I have also witnessed quinceañera services in Methodist, Baptist, and nondenominational churches.

3. Here I am thinking of the matachines dance ritual or the many saint devotions that include processions and special rituals for the feast day. See Cantú (2009).

4. The age of 15 is critical, for that was the age when a woman in Mexico could marry without her parents' consent. My paternal grandmother married at 15, as was the custom in the early twentieth century.

5. See *SB4 (Senate Bill 4) Law Quinceañera Protest*, MTV News (2017).

6. See Julia Alvarez's *Once Upon a Quinceañera: Coming of Age in the USA* (2007) for a take on various celebrations in the United States by Latinx immigrant communities.
7. Coatlicue is the Mexica goddess of death and rebirth. Anzaldúa ([1987] 1999) describes a Coatlicue state as a mental paralysis that portends transformation.

Notes for Chapter 3

1. A quick review of the announcements for the festivals in the parishes in Laredo reveal that they are still called *jamaicas*, although some change seems to be underway to call them *kermes*.
2. See Roxanne Dunbar-Ortiz's book, *Not "A Nation of Immigrants": Settler Colonialism, White Supremacy, and a History of Erasure and Exclusion* (2021) for further discussion of settler colonialism in the United States.
3. I refer readers (as Peña does) to Woolridge and Vezzetti's "Founding of Charro Days" (1989) and to Knopp, Medrano, and Rodriguez, *Charro Days in Brownsville* (2009). Also, for more on transborder festivals along the Texas-Tamaulipas border, see Oliveras-González's "Fiestas transfronterizas y representaciones espaciales en la frontera México-Texas" (2016). Buccaneer Days started in 1938, modeled after a Spanish royal court, and pays homage to Alonso De Piñeda, who "discovered" Corpus Christi Bay. While similar in that it, too, has the daughters of the elites in town presented by the Las Doñas de la Corte, it is an even stranger phenomenon, as it is a Spanish Court that is represented and the mostly white participants enact a court that never happened, in fact elevating de Piñeda to a monarch, a monarch who never existed—or rather not a reference to Rey Alonso.
4. See Laura D. Gutiérrez's article "'Trains of Misery': Repatriate Voices and Responses in Northern Mexico during the Great Depression" (2020) and Fernando Saúl Alanís Enciso's *They*

Should Stay There: The Story of Mexican Migration and Repatriation during the Great Depression (2017).

5. See two biographies for more information on this colorful political and military figure who served as president of the Republic of Texas between Sam Houston's two terms. Jack C. Ramsay's *Thunder beyond the Brazos: A Biography of Mirabeau B. Lamar* (1985) and Stanley Siegel's *The Poet President of Texas: The Life of Mirabeau B. Lamar, President of the Republic of Texas* (1977).

6. See McNeely and Kleiner (1994) for more information about the antimony smelter.

7. For more on García Canclini's ideas about the hybridity of culture, see García Canclini 2009.

8. See Elliott Young's (1998) article for an explanation of the social strata catered to by each—the Pokies or the Marthas, as they are commonly referred to in the local idioms.

9. The Laredo Crime Stoppers, Inc., was founded in 1981 and remains active as a nonprofit organization that exists, as their website states, "for the specific and primary purpose to obtain information about crimes, wanted persons and criminal activities; to help develop a community offensive against crime; to motivate members of the public to cooperate with law enforcement agencies; and to provide for rewards and award such cooperation." It is a crime-control program that "provides resources necessary for concerned citizens to solve crimes which make them eligible for a cash reward up to $1,000.00" ("Home," 2022). The Menudo Bowl is their primary fundraising event.

10. Conservas La Costeña is the brand name commonly known as La Costeña. The Mexican company's canned products—including jalapeño peppers—can be found in supermarkets all over the United States.

11. For more information see Simon Romero's (2019) article in the *New York Times*, "La Gordiloca: The Swearing Muckraker Upending Border Journalism."

Notes for Conclusion

1. Although the term exists in Spanish, especially the Spanish of South Texas, as a term that describes maneuvers or strategies to accomplish a desired outcome, I take the term from the book *Chicana Movidas: New Narratives of Feminism and Activism in the Movement* (Espinoza, Cotera, and Blackwell 2018), where it is more in line with a Chicana feminist project to counter the patriarchal narrative of the Chicano Movement. See the coeditors' "Introduction: Movement, Movimientos and Movidas."

2. Prof. Stanley Green says as much in a TikTok video featured in the Webb County Heritage Foundation Society's web page (2022c).

References

Alanís Enciso, Fernando Saúl. 2017. *They Should Stay There: The Story of Mexican Migration and Repatriation during the Great Depression*. Translated by Russ Davidson. Latin America in Translation. Chapel Hill: University of North Carolina Press.

Alvarez, Julia. 2007. *Once upon a Quinceañera: Coming of Age in the USA*. New York: Viking.

Anzaldúa, Gloria. (1987) 2019. *Borderlands / La Frontera: The New Mestiza*. San Francisco: Spinsters / Aunt Lute Books.

Anzaldúa, Gloria E. 2002. "Preface: (Un)natural bridges, (Un)safe spaces." In Anzaldúa and Keating 2002, 1–5.

Anzaldúa, Gloria E. 2002. "now let us shift . . . the path of conocimiento . . . inner work, public acts." In Anzaldúa and Keating 2002, 540–78.

Anzaldúa, Gloria E., and AnaLouise Keating, eds. 2002. *This Bridge We Call Home: Radical Visions for Transformation*. New York: Routledge.

Arreola, Daniel D., and James R. Curtis. 1994. *The Mexican Border Cities: Landscape Anatomy and Place Personality*. Tucson: University of Arizona Press.

"At What Age Is the Brain Fully Developed?" n.d. *Mental Health Daily*. Accessed October 11, 2022. https://mentalhealthdaily.com/2015/02/18/at-what-age-is-the-brain-fully-developed/.

Barrera, Cordelia E. 2022. *The Haunted Southwest: Towards an Ethics of Place in Borderlands Literature*. Lubbock: Texas Tech University Press.

Bary, Leslie. 2021. "Border Trouble: Anzaldúa's Margins." In *Intersectional Feminism in the Age of Transnationalism: Voices from the Margins*, edited by Olga Bezhanova and Raysa E. Amador, 41–83. Lanham, MD: Lexington Books.

Behar, Ruth. 1996. *The Vulnerable Observer: Anthropology That Breaks Your Heart*. Boston: Beacon Press.

Benavides, Norma Zuñiga, and Blanca Zuñiga Azíos. 1995. *Holidays and Heartstrings: Recuerdos de La Casa de Miel*. Laredo, TX: Border Studies.

Bhabha, Homi K. 2004. *The Location of Culture*. 2nd ed. London: Routledge.

Bhattacharya, Kakali. 2020. "Autohistoria-teoría: Merging Self, Culture, Community, Spirit, and Theory." *Journal of Autoethnography* 1 (2): 198–202. https://doi.org/10.1525/joae.2020.1.2.198.

Botello, Robert. 2022. *We Dance for the Virgen: Authenticity of Tradition in a San Antonio Matachines Troupe*. College Station: Texas A&M Press.

Brandes, Stanley. 1988. *Power and Persuasion: Fiestas and Social Control in Rural Mexico*. Philadelphia: University of Pennsylvania Press. https://doi.org/10.9783/9780812292497.

Bryant, Miranda. 2016. "Is This America's Luckiest Teenager? Father Throws 15-Year-Old Daughter a $6 MILLION Quinceañera with Nick Jonas, Pitbull, Make-up by the Kardashians' Artist and Photos by Michelle Obama's Photographer." *Daily Mail Online*. March 9, 2016. https://www.dailymail.co.uk/femail/article-3483958/Is-America-s-luckiest-teenager-15-year-old-girl-thrown-lavish-6-MILLION-Quincea-era-performances-Nick-Jonas-Pitbull-make-Kardashians-artist-pictures-Michelle-Obama-s-photographer.html.

Cantú, Norma E. 1999. "La Quinceañera: Towards an Ethnographic Analysis of a Life-Cycle Ritual." *Southern Folklore* 56 (1): 73–101.

Cantú, Norma E. 2002. "Chicana Life Cycle Rituals." In *Chicana Traditions: Continuity and Change*, edited by Norma E. Cantú and Olga Nájera-Ramírez, 15–34. Urbana-Champaign: University of Illinois Press.

Cantú, Norma E. 2009. "The Semiotics of Land and Place: Matachines Dancing in Laredo, Texas." In *Dancing across Borders: Danzas y Bailes Mexicanos*, edited by Olga Nájera-Ramírez, Norma Elia Cantú, and Brenda M Romero, 97–115. Urbana: University of Illinois Press.

Cantú, Norma E. 2010. "Traditional Cultural Expressions: An Analysis of the Religious and Secular Folkways of Latin@s in the United States." In *Inside the Latin@ Experience: A Latin@ Studies Reader*, edited by Norma E. Cantú and María E. Fránquiz, 111–28. New York: Palgrave Macmillan.

Cantú, Norma E. 2011. "*Dos Mundos* [Two Worlds]: Two Celebrations in Laredo, Texas—Los Matachines de La Santa Cruz and the Pocahontas Pageant of the George Washington's Birthday Celebration." In *Global Mexican Cultural Productions*, edited by Rosana Blanco Cano and Rita Urquijo-Ruiz, 61–74. New York: Palgrave Macmillan.

Cantú, Norma E. 2012. "Performing Indigeneity in a South Texas Community: Los Matachines de La Santa Cruz." In *Performing the US Latina and Latino Borderlands*, edited by Arturo J. Aldama, Chela Sandoval, and Peter J. García, 127–45. Bloomington: Indiana University Press.

Cantú, Norma E. 2014. "'Quinceañeras and Cincuentañeras.'" In *Encyclopedia of Latino Culture: From Calaveras to Quinceañeras*, edited by Charles M. Tatum, 1:283–88. Santa Barbara, CA: Greenwood Press.

Cantú, Norma E. n.d. "Los Matachines de La Santa Cruz de La Ladrillera." *National Endowment for the Arts*. Accessed August 29, 2022. https://www.arts.gov/honors/heritage/los-matachines-de-la-santa-cruz-de-la-ladrillera.

Cervantes, Lorna Dee. 1981. *Emplumada*. Pittsburgh: University of Pittsburgh Press.

Cota-Robles Newton, Frank, and Rene A. Ruiz. 1981 "Chicano Culture and Mental Health Among the Elderly." In *Chicano Aging and Mental Health*, edited by Manuel Miranda and Rene A. Ruiz, 38–75. San Francisco: Human Resources Corp.

Crenshaw, Kimberlé. 1989. "Demarginalizing the Intersection of Race and Sex: A Black Feminist Critique of Antidiscrimination Doctrine, Feminist Theory and Antiracist Politics." *University of Chicago Legal Forum* 1989: 139–68.

Davalos, Karen Mary. 1996. "'La Quinceañera': Making Gender and Ethnic Identities." *Frontiers: A Journal of Women Studies* 16 (2/3): 101–27. https://doi.org/10.2307/3346805.

de Beauvoir, Simone. 1953. *The Second Sex*. Translated by H. M. Parshley. New York: Knopf.

de Hoyos, Angela. 1977. *Chicano Poems: For the Barrio*. San Antonio: M & A Editions.

De la Teja, Jesús F. 1998. "The Camino Real: Colonial Texas' Lifeline to the World." In *A Texas Legacy: The Old San Antonio Road and the Caminos Reales, A Tricentennial History, 1691–1991*, edited by Joachim McGraw, John W. Clark Jr., and Elizabeth A. Robbins, 43–48. 2nd ed. Austin: Texas Department of Transportation.

Diaz, Thatiana. 2017. "Quinceañera Protests against Texas Anti-Immigration Bill." *People.* July 18, 2017. https://people.com/chica/quinceanera-protest-texas-anti-immigration-bill/.

Dunbar-Ortiz, Roxanne. 2021. *Not "A Nation of Immigrants": Settler Colonialism, White Supremacy, and a History of Erasure and Exclusion.* Boston: Beacon Press.

Durán, Diego. 1994. *The History of the Indies of New Spain.* Translated by Doris Heyden. Civilization of the American Indian Series. Norman: University of Oklahoma Press.

Erevia, Angela. 1980. *Religious Celebration for the Quinceañera.* San Antonio: Mexican American Cultural Center.

Erevia, Angela. 1985. *Quince Años: Celebrating a Tradition / Celebrando un [sic] Tradición.* San Antonio, TX: Missionary Catechists of Divine Providence.

Erevia, Angela. (1992) 1996. *Quince Años: Celebrating a Tradition—A Handbook for Parish Teams.* San Antonio, TX: Missionary Catechists of Divine Providence.

Espinoza, Dionne, María Eugenia Cotera, and Maylei Blackwell. 2018. *Chicana Movidas: New Narratives of Activism and Feminism in the Movement.* Austin: University of Texas Press.

"Events—WBCA." 2022. Washington's Birthday Celebration Association. 2022. https://wbcalaredo.org/events/.

Fanon, Frantz. 1967. *Black Skin, White Masks.* Translated by Charles Lam Markmann. New York: Grove Press.

Fierros, Cindy O., and Dolores Delgado Bernal. 2016. "Vamos a Placticar: The Contours of Pláticas as Chicana/Latina Feminist Methodology." *Chicana/Latina Studies* 15 (2): 98–121.

Firestone, Shulamith. 1970. *The Dialectic of Sex: The Case for Feminist Revolution.* New York: William Morrow.

Frye, Northrop. 1957. *Anatomy of Criticism: Four Essays.* Princeton: Princeton University Press.

Garcia, Josephine Worsham. n.d. "The Coal Mines." Unpublished Manuscript. Laredo Public Library.

García Canclini, Néstor. 1995. *Consumidores y ciudadanos: Conflictos multiculturales de la globalización.* Mexico City: Grijalbo.

García Canclini, Néstor. 2009. *Culturas híbridas: Estrategias para entrar y salir de la modernidad.* México, D.F.: Random House Mondadori.

Geertz, Clifford. (1973) 2017. *The Interpretation of Cultures*. New York: Basic Books.

González, Jovita. 1927. *Folk-lore of the Texas-Mexican Vaquero*. Austin: Texas Folk-lore Society.

González, Rachel Valentina. 2019. *Quinceañera Style: Social Belonging and Latinx Consumer Identities*. Austin: University of Texas Press.

González, Teresita. 2021. Personal Interview. Laredo, TX. May 27.

González-Martin, Rachel Valentina. 2020. "Buying the Dream: Relating 'Traditional' Dress to Consumer Practices in US Quinceañeras." In *MeXicana Fashions: Politics, Self-Adornment, and Identity Construction*, edited by Aída Hurtado and Norma E. Cantú, 137–57. Austin: University of Texas Press.

Graham, Joe S. 1992. *Hecho en Tejas: Texas-Mexican Folk Arts and Crafts*. Publications of the Texas Folklore Society 50. Lubbock: University of North Texas Press.

Grajeda, Rafael Francisco. 1974. "The Figure of the Pocho in Contemporary Chicano Fiction." PhD diss., University of Nebraska–Lincoln. https://www.proquest.com/docview/288355640/citation/DA683C59840547A2PQ/1.

Gramsci, Antonio. 1973. *Selections from the Prison Notebooks of Antonio Gramsci*. Edited by Quintin Hoare and Geoffrey Nowell-Smith. New York: International Publishers.

Green, Stanley C. 1991a. *A Celebration of Heritage*. Laredo, TX: Border Studies.

Green, Stanley C. 1991b. *Laredo 1755–1920: An Overview*. Laredo, TX: Border Studies.

Green, Stanley C. 1992. *A History of the Washington Birthday Celebration*. Laredo, TX: Border Studies.

Green, Stanley C. 1993. *Border Biographies: Illustrated*. 2nd ed. Laredo, TX: Border Studies.

Gutiérrez, Laura D. 2020. "'Trains of Misery': Repatriate Voices and Responses in Northern Mexico during the Great Depression." *Journal of American Ethnic History* 39 (4): 13–26. https://doi.org/10.5406/jamerethnhist.39.4.0013.

Harris, Max. 1994. "The Arrival of the Europeans: Folk Dramatizations of the Conquest and Conversion in New Mexico." *Comparative Drama* 28 (1): 141–65.

Harris, Max. 1997. "The Return of Moctezuma: Oaxaca's 'Danza de La Pluma' and New Mexico's 'Danza de Los Matachines.'" *TDR* 41 (1): 106–34. https://doi.org/10.2307/1146575.

Harris, Max. 2000. *Aztecs, Moors, and Christians: Festivals of Reconquest in Mexico and Spain*. Austin: University of Texas.

Herman, Lily. 2017. "Quinceañera Held at Texas Capitol Building." *Teen Vogue*. July 19, 2017. https://www.teenvogue.com/story/quinceanera-held-at-texas-capitol-building.

Hernández Tovar, Inés. 1978. *Con Razón Corazón*. San Antonio: M & A Editions.

"History." n.d. *WBCA Laredo*. Accessed October 24, 2022. https://wbcalaredo.org/history/, https://wbcalaredo.org/history/.

"Home." 2022. Laredo Crime Stoppers. 2022. https://www.laredo-crimestoppers.org.

Hurtado, Aída. 1997. "Understanding Multiple Group Identities: Inserting Women into Cultural Transformations." *Journal of Social Issues* 53 (2): 299–327. https://doi.org/10.1111/j.1540-4560.1997.tb02445.x.

Ibarra, Cristina, dir. 2014. *Las Marthas*. Documentary, History. Undocumented Films.

Jaramillo, Cleofas M. 1972. *Shadows of the Past / Sombras Del Pasado*. Santa Fe: Ancient City Press.

Kingsley, Gina. 2015. "A Peruvian Quinceanera in Tulsa." *Gypsy Family Travel* (blog). November 24, 2015. https://www.gypsy-familytravel.com/a-quinceanera-in-tulsa/.

Knopp, Anthony K., Manuel Medrano, Priscilla Rodriguez, and the Brownsville Historical Association. 2009. *Charro Days in Brownsville*. Images of America. Charleston, SC: Arcadia.

"Laredo's 2022 Menudo Bowl Postponed Due to COVID Spike." 2022. *Laredo Morning Times*. January 11, 2022. https://www.lmton-line.com/news/article/Laredo-s-2022-Menudo-Bowl-postponed-due-to-16767959.php.

Latina Feminist Collective. 2001. *Telling to Live: Latina Feminist Testimonios*. Latin America Otherwise. Durham: Duke University Press.

Lea, Aurora Lucero-White. 1953. *Literary Folklore of the Hispanic Southwest*. San Antonio: Naylor.

León Portilla, Miguel. 1990. *Aztec Thought and Culture: A Study of the Ancient Nahuatl Mind.* Civilization of the American Indian Series. Norman: University of Oklahoma Press.

Lugones, María. 2007. "Heterosexualism and the Colonial/ Modern Gender System." *Hypatia* 22 (1): 186–209. https://doi. org/10.1111/j.1527-2001.2007.tb01156.x.

Lugones, María. 2010. "Toward a Decolonial Feminism." *Hypatia* Special Issue: Feminist Legacies / Feminist Futures 25 (4): 742–59. https://doi.org/10.1111/j.1527-2001.2010.01137.x.

Luna, Rudy, and Enrique Alemán Jr. 2013. *Stolen Education.* DVD. Documentary, Drama. AlemanLuna Productions.

Maldonado, David, Jr. 1975. "The Chicano Aged." *Social Work* 20 (3): 213–16. https://doi.org/10.1093/sw/20.3.213.

Manning, Frank E. 1992. "Spectacle." In *Folklore, Cultural Performances, and Popular Entertainments: A Communications-Centered Handbook,* edited by Richard Bauman, 291–99. New York: Oxford University Press.

McNeely, John H., and Diana J. Kleiner. 1994. "Antimony Smelter." In *Handbook of Texas.* Texas State Historical Association. https://www.tshaonline.org/handbook/entries/antimony-smelter.

Medina, Néstor. 2009. *Mestizaje: (Re)Mapping Race, Culture, and Faith in Latina/o Catholicism.* Maryknoll, NY: Orbis Books.

Mignolo, Walter D. 2000. *Local Histories/Global Designs: Coloniality, Subaltern Knowledges, and Border Thinking.* Princeton Studies in Culture, Power, History. Princeton: Princeton University Press.

Mignolo, Walter D. 2012. *Local Histories/Global Designs: Coloniality, Subaltern Knowledges, and Border Thinking.* Princeton: Princeton University Press.

Mignolo, Walter D. n.d. "Worlds & Knowledges Otherwise." Duke Center for Global Studies and the Humanities. Accessed September 28, 2022. https://globalstudies.trinity.duke.edu/projects/worlds.

Mignolo, Walter D., and Gabriela Nouzeil. 2003. "Editorial Note: From *Nepantla* to *Worlds and Knowledges Otherwise.*" *Nepantla: Views from the South* 4 (3): 421–22.

Montejano, David. 1987. *Anglos and Mexicans in the Making of Texas, 1836–1986.* Austin: University of Texas Press.

Moraga, Cherríe. 1986. *Giving up the Ghost: Teatro in Two Acts*. Los Angeles, CA: West End Press.

Moraga, Cherríe, and Gloria Anzaldúa. 2002. *This Bridge Called My Back: Writings by Radical Women of Color*. 3rd ed. Women of Color Series. Berkeley, CA: Third Woman Press.

MTV News, dir. 2017. *SB4 (Senate Bill 4) Law Quinceañera Protest*. https://www.youtube.com/watch?v=aJQ7J240dXw.

Mulcahy, Joanne. 2011. *Remedios: The Healing Life of Eva Castellanoz*. New York: Trinity University Press.

"Nor Gara." 2020. *Olentzerozaleen Elkartea*. Accessed September 28, 2022. https://olentzero.net/nor-gara/.

Oliveras-González, Xavier. 2016. "Fiestas transfronterizas y representaciones espaciales en la frontera México-Texas." *Economía, Sociedad y Territorio* 16 (50): 133–69.

Paredes, Américo. 1976. *A Texas-Mexican Cancionero: Folksongs of the Lower Border*. Music in American Life. Urbana: University of Illinois Press.

Peña, Alfonso Felix. 1972. "Los Matachines." Unpublished manuscript. Laredo Public Library.

Peña, Elaine A. 2020. *¡Viva George! Celebrating Washington's Birthday at the US-Mexico Border*. Jack and Doris Smothers Series in Texas History, Life, and Culture 49. Austin: University of Texas Press.

Pérez, Emma. 1999. *The Decolonial Imaginary: Writing Chicanas into History*. Bloomington: Indiana University Press.

Primera, Maye, and Almudena Toral. 2016. "Rubi's 'Quinceañera': Mexico Gets a Viral Lesson." *Univision*. December 31, 2016. https://www.univision.com/univision-news/culture/rubis-quinceanera-mexico-gets-a-viral-lesson.

Quijano, Aníbal. 1991. "Colonialidad y racionalidad/modernidad." *Perú Indigena* 13 (29): 11–29.

Quijano, Aníbal. 2001/2002. "Colonialidad Del Poder, Globalización y Democracia." *Revista de Ciencias Sociales de La Universidad Autónoma de Nuevo León* 4 (7–8): 1–23.

"Quinceañera." 2019. *Holy Family Church*. https://holyfamily.org/quinceanera/.

Ramsay, Jack C. 1985. *Thunder beyond the Brazos: A Biography of Mirabeau B. Lamar*. Austin: Eakin Press.

Rappaport, Roy A. 1992. "Ritual." In *Folklore, Cultural Performances, and Popular Entertainments: A Communications-Centered*

Handbook, edited by Richard Bauman, 249–60. New York: Oxford University Press.

Rendón, Laura I. 2014. *Sentipensante (Sensing/Thinking) Pedagogy: Educating for Wholeness, Social Justice and Liberation*. Sterling, VA: Stylus.

Rich, Adrienne. 1979. *On Lies, Secrets, and Silence: Selected Prose, 1966–1978*. New York: W. W. Norton.

Richardson, Marlene, producer. 1996. "Los Matachines de La Santa Cruz de La Ladrillera." San Antonio: KLRN; Alamo Public Telecommunications Council.

Rodríguez, Sylvia. 1994. "Defended Boundaries, Precarious Elites: The Arroyo Seco Matachines Dance." *Journal of American Folklore* 107 (424): 248–67. https://doi.org/10.2307/541203.

Rodríguez, Sylvia. 1996. *The Matachines Dance: Ritual Symbolism and Interethnic Relations in the Rio Grande Valley*. Albuquerque: University of New Mexico Press.

Rodríguez, Sylvia. 2009. *The Matachines Dance: A Ritual Dance of the Indian Pueblos and Mexicano/Hispano Communities*. Santa Fe: Sunstone Press.

Romero, Brenda M. 1993. "The Matachines Music and Dance in San Juan Pueblo and Alcalde, New Mexico: Contexts and Meanings." PhD diss., University of California–Los Angeles. https://www.proquest.com/docview/304055669/abstract/6413 642E108342DFPQ/1.

Romero, Brenda M. 1997. "Cultural Interaction in New Mexico as Illustrated in the Matachines Dance." *Musics of Multicultural America: A Study of Twelve Musical Communities*, edited by Kip Lornell and Anne K. Rasmussen, 155–85. New York: Schirmer.

Romero, Brenda M. 1999. "Old World Origins of the Matachines Dance." In *Vistas of American Music: Essays and Compositions in Honor of William K. Kearns*, edited by Susan L. Porter and John Graziano, 339–56. Detroit Monographs in Musicology 25. Warren, MI: Harmonie Park Press.

Romero, Simon. 2019. "La Gordiloca: The Swearing Muckraker Upending Border Journalism." *New York Times*, March 10, 2019. https://www.nytimes.com/2019/03/10/us/gordiloca-laredo-priscilla-villarreal.html.

Salcedo, Michele. 1997. *Quinceañera! The Essential Guide to Planning the Perfect Sweet Fifteen Celebration*. New York: Henry Holt.

Sandoval, Chela. 1991. "U.S. Third World Feminism: The Theory and Method of Oppositional Consciousness in the Postmodern World." *Genders* 10 (March):1–24. https://doi.org/10.5555/gen.1991.10.1.

Sandoval, Chela. 2000. *Methodology of the Oppressed*. Theory out of Bounds. Minneapolis: University of Minnesota Press.

Scott, James C. 1992. *Domination and the Arts of Resistance: Hidden Transcripts*. New Haven: Yale University Press.

Siegel, Stanley. 1977. *The Poet President of Texas: The Life of Mirabeau B. Lamar, President of the Republic of Texas*. Presidents and Governors of Texas Series. Austin: Jenkins.

Sotomayor, Marta. 1971. "Mexican American Interaction with Social Systems." *Social Casework* 52 (5): 316–22.

Stoeltje, Beverly J. 1992. "Festival." In *Folklore, Cultural Performances, and Popular Entertainments: A Communications-Centered Handbook*, edited by Richard Bauman, 261–71. New York: Oxford University Press.

Thompson, Jerry D. 1986. *Laredo: A Pictorial History*. Norfolk: Donning.

Thompson, Jerry D. 1991. *Warm Weather and Bad Whiskey: The 1886 Laredo Election Riot*. El Paso: Texas Western Press.

Thompson, Jerry D., ed. 2011. *Tejanos in Gray: Civil War Letters of Captains Joseph Rafael de La Garza and Manuel Yturri*. Translated by José Roberto Juárez. Fronteras Series. College Station: Texas A&M University Press.

Thompson, Jerry D. 2015. *A Civil War History of the New Mexico Volunteers and Militia*. Albuquerque: University of New Mexico Press.

Thompson, Jerry D. 2017. *Tejano Tiger: José de Los Santos Benavides and the Texas-Mexico Borderlands, 1823–1891*. TCU Texas Biography Series. Fort Worth: TCU Press.

Treviño, Adrian, and Barbara Gilles. 1994. "A History of the Matachines Dance." *New Mexico Historical Review* 69 (2): 105–125. https://digitalrepository.unm.edu/nmhr/vol69/iss2/2

Tyx, Daniel Blue. 2019. "Washington Crossing the Rio Grande." *Texas Observer*, June 10, 2019. https://www.texasobserver.org/washington-crossing-the-rio-grande/.

United States Conference of Catholic Bishops. 2007. "Bendición al Cumplir Quince Años: Order for the Blessing on the Fifteenth

Birthday." https://richmonddiocese.org/wp-content/uploads/2015/10/Bilingual-Ritual-Quinceanera.pdf.

Valderas, Alejandro. 2009. *El ramo de Navidad*. Biblioteca leonesa de tradiciones. Trobajo del Camino, León: Edilesa.

Van Gennep, Arnold. 1960. *The Rites of Passage*. Translated by Monika G. Vizedom and Gabrielle L. Caffee. Chicago: University of Chicago Press.

Vela, Jorge A. 2021. "The Jalapeno Festival Is Back as Lineup Is Announced." *Laredo Morning Times*. November 14, 2021. https://www.lmtonline.com/news/article/The-Jalapeno-Festival-is-back-as-lineup-is-16620366.php.

Vigil-Piñón, Evangelina. 1978. *Nade y Nade: A Collection of Poems*. San Antonio: M & A Editions.

Webb County Heritage Society. 2022a. "Why Do We Celebrate George Washington's Birthday in Laredo?" TikTok. February 15, 2022. https://www.tiktok.com/@webbheritage/video/706499011294139 5246.

Webb County Heritage Society. 2022b. "How Has the George Washington's Celebration Changed?" TikTok. February 15, 2022. https://www.tiktok.com/@webbheritage/video/7065069805132467503.

Webb County Heritage Society. 2022c. "Why Do We Still Celebrate George Washington's Birthday?" TikTok. February 17, 2022. https://www.tiktok.com/@webbheritage/video/7065741357847153966.

Woolridge, Ruby, and Robert B. Vezzetti. 1989. "The Founding of Charro Days." In *More Studies in Brownsville History*, edited by Milo Kearney, 390–91. Brownsville: University of Texas at Brownsville.

Young, Elliott. 1994. "Deconstructing 'La Raza': Identifying the 'Gente Decente' of Laredo, 1904–1911." *Southwestern Historical Quarterly* 98 (2): 227–59.

Young, Elliott. 1998. "Red Men, Princess Pocahontas, and George Washington: Harmonizing Race Relations in Laredo at the Turn of the Century." *Western Historical Quarterly* 29 (1): 49–85. https://doi.org/10.2307/970806.

Zamora, Bernice, and José Antonio Burciaga. 1976. *Restless Serpents*. Menlo Park, CA: Diseños Literarios.

Index

L

La Joya, San Luis Potosi, 77
La Ladrillera (barrio), 29, 36
La Lucha, 52
La Mancha, Spain, 45
Lamar, Mirabeau B., 95, 127
La Posada Hotel, 3, 100
Lara, Luis Antonio, 106
Laredo Air Force Base, 81, 90, 121
Laredo Civic Center, 108
Laredo College, 5, 83, 98
Laredo Junior College, 5
Laredo Police Department, 115
Laredo Public Library, 4, 124
Laredo State University, 8, 25,
 34, 97
Las Minas, 23, 29, 32–34, 49
Latinx culture, 61, 72–73, 80, 126
Lent, 2
Liendo
 Carolina, 44, 124
 Claudina, 39–40, 124
 Leonides, 35
 Sarita, 21, 24, 33, 35, 39–40, 42,
 45, 124
Liendo Vigil, Gloria, 45
Ligarde, Honoré, 92
Lipan Apache, 27
Liu, Terry, 9
Lomax Hawes, Bess, 9
Lugones, María, 16, 120
LULAC, 93

M

Madrid, Spain, 8, 24
madrinas, 64, 66, 68–70, 72
 madrina de bouquet, 70
 madrina de medulla, 64
 madrina de última muñeca, 69

madrina de zapatos, 66, 68
 See also padrinos
Malinche, 28
las mañanitas, 70
mantilla, 72
manzanilla, 6, 33
mariachi, 6, 70, 77
Martha Washington Colonial Ball,
 91, 101–2, 109–10
Las Martas (film), photo gallery
Martin High School, 91, 108
matachines, 2, 5, 8–11, 13–15, 17,
 21–38, 41–42, 44–47, 49, 52,
 93, 102–4, 122, 124–25
 Danza de Matachines, 37, 124
 Matachines de la Santa Cruz de la
 Ladrillera, 24, 29–32, 46, 93
McDonald's, 100
McGraw, Tim, 66
menudo, 100, 104–7, 127
Menudo Bowl Cook-Off, 104–5
Mescalero Apache, 74
mestizaje, 26, 124
 mestizo culture, 44, 94, 111, 120
Mexico, 11–12, 23, 26–29, 46,
 54, 62, 64, 71–72, 77, 82, 85,
 88–89, 124–26
 Central Mexico, 71–72, 77
 Northern Mexico, 11, 23, 26–27,
 29, 54, 101, 126
Mignolo, Walter D., 58, 120
Miller Lite, 100
Minera, Texas, 29
mojigangas, 5, 34
mole, 41, 77, 104
Monarca, 28
Montezuma, 28
Mother Cabrini Church, 11, 22–23, 36
movidas, 120, 128